Published by Writer's Publishing House
writerspublishinghouse.com

Cover Created by Writer's Publishing House Staff

The Ultimate Teenager's Guide to Success
Transformation Through Self- Education

carmichaellewis.com

ISBN 978-1-952274-00-8

Carmichael Lewis Copyright © 2020 All Rights Reserved

All rights reserved. No part of this book may be reproduced in whole or in part, without the written permission of the publisher except by a reviewer who may quote brief passages in a review; nor may any part of this book be reproduced or transmitted in any form or by any means, electronic or mechanical, including photocopying recording, or by any information storage and retrieval system, without the written permission of the publisher.

The Ultimate Teenager's Guide to Success:

By Carmichael Lewis

Disclaimer

The author has made every effort to ensure the accuracy of the information within this book was correct at the time of publication. The author does not assume and hereby disclaims any liability to any party for any loss, damage, or disruption caused by errors or omissions, whether such errors or omissions result from accident, negligence, or any other cause.

The information contained within this Book/eBook is strictly for educational purposes. If you wish to apply ideas contained in this Book/eBook, you are taking full responsibility for your actions.

Disclaimer: The Publisher and the Author make no representation or warranties with respect to the accuracy or completeness of the contents of this work and specifically disclaim all warranties for a particular purpose. No warranty may be created or extended by sales or promotional materials. The advice and strategies contained herein may not be suitable for every situation. This work is sold with the understanding that the publisher is not engaged in rendering legal, accounting, or other professional services. If professional assistance is required, the services of a competent professional person should be sought. Neither the Publisher nor the Author shall be liable for damages arising therefrom.

The fact that an organization or website is referred to in this work as a citation and/or potential source of further information does not mean that the Author or the Publisher endorses the information, the organization, or website it may provide or recommendations it may make. Further, readers should be aware that websites listed in this work may have changed or disappeared between when this work was written and when it is read. The cases and stories in this book have had details changed to preserve privacy.

Table of Contents

Disclaimer 3

Introduction 10

    How to Use This Book 14

Section One 15

    Decided Who You Want to Be 15

        Create a Vision for Your Life 16

        You Can't Be What You Don't See 19

        The S.M.A.R.T Way to Plan 24

        Short vs. Long-Term Planning 28

        You Always Need Another Plan A 29

        Success Requires Sacrifice 30

        Manage Your Time 33

        Don't Give Up. EVER. 34

Section Two 38

    Choose the Right School 38

        Free Money: Finding Grants and Scholarships 44

        Become a Resident Assistant and Live on Campus for Free 45

Skills That Pay Bills (Sports) 47

I am An Upper Classman, I Got This! 49

Who Is Your Mentor? 50

Who Is Your Mentee? 52

Get Involved 54

What Options Do I Have Besides College? 56

What About Going Into The Military? 56

What Makes You Happy? 58

Section Three 61

How Are You Representing Yourself? 63

Attitude is Everything! 66

Invest in Yourself 68

Be Helpful 70

Section Four 72

Get Your Mind Right 72

Be Your Own Hero 73

Morning Motivation 75

Affirming Yourself 76

Practice Gratitude 77

Meditation for the mind 78

Guard Your Mind 80

Section Five 84

  Keep Your Emotions in Check 84

    Anger Management: A Quick Lesson 84

    Don't Sweat the Small Things 87

    Bullying is Never Tolerated 89

Section Six 93

  Value Your Relationships 93

    Respect Your Elders 93

    Respect Your Friends 95

    The Crowd You Keep 96

    The Person with No Goals 100

    Let's Talk About Dating 102

    Keep Your Hands to Yourself 106

Section Seven 107

  Get Your Body Right 107

Section Eight 113

  Social Media Dos and Don'ts 113

    Represent Yourself Well Online 113

    Be in the moment 118

Section Nine 120

   I Have My Driver's License, How Do I Keep It? 120

      Driving While Distracted: Don't Do It! 120

      Why the Earbuds? 122

      What Are You Listening to That Is So Important? 123

      Just Say No! 126

      Be Someone Your Parents Can Trust 129

      Interacting with a Police Officer 132

      You Need Insurance 138

      Full Coverage Insurance 139

Section Ten 141

   Making Your Own Money 141

      Work Part-Time While in School 141

      What Does Your Email Say About You? 145

      Preparing for your job interview 146

      Dress Like You Want the Job 149

      Great Companies to Work For 150

      Start Your Own Business 152

      Start Small but Dream Big 152

      Start a Bike Rental Business 153

Start a Video Game System Rental Business 153

Start a Cleaning Business.. 154

Start a Landscaping Business.. 154

Start a Car Wash Business 155

Get Paid to Take Surveys.. 156

Get Paid to Deliver Groceries 157

Get Paid to Save.. 157

Buy and Sell Domain Names.. 157

Think About a Real Estate Business................................... 158

Section Eleven 159

Get Your Money Right 159

You Need A Budget.. 161

Stop Spending So Much.. 165

Save A Little 167

Have an Emergency Fund... 168

Are you Ready to Have Your Own Car? 171

You Don't Have to Impress 173

Checking and Savings Accounts... 175

Now That You Have a Job, this is What You Need to Know!
.... 178

Home and Renters Insurance 183

Live Debt Free 184

What is Interest? 187

How to Avoid Interest... 188

Financial Independence 189

How to Grow Wealth 191

Find the Right Property and Team.. 192

Making an Offer... 192

Do the Math 194

House Hack... 194

Becoming a Real Estate Investor 195

Positives and The Negatives About Investing. 201

Invest in Your Community 202

You Got This! 206

About the Author 210

Introduction

When you hear an interview with a successful person, one of the most common questions asked is "What advice would you give your younger self?" The responses may be different depending on the person asked, but you may hear things ranging from Find a mentor, save more money, don't be afraid to go after your dreams. All these answers are right and usually practical. And they are based on real-world experience, instead of what we are taught in school.

Now, don't get me wrong—school is valuable. The math, English, and history you're learning now is a foundation you can build on to help you succeed in college and beyond. School helps you to expand your mind, learn discipline, create study habits, and meet people outside of your community. You should listen and learn everything you can. But even with everything your teachers and textbooks teach you, there is still so much more they don't.

That is why I wrote this book for you—and for the me.

I was an alright student, but I was hardheaded. I stayed in trouble, and I made far too many decisions I am not proud of. My life was much harder than it had to be. But with all my mistakes, I always knew I wanted more for myself and that education, knowledge and exposure were the keys to my success. Even though, I failed the 6th grade I was the first sibling to go to college. I have two degrees, a bachelor's, and a Master's. I am the founder of a fitness clothing brand. I teach people how to live a healthier lifestyle as a personal trainer. I have invested in real estate that generates thousands of dollars in additional income every month. And, as I am writing this book, I've been a police officer with the Chicago Police Department for seven years. I have spent five years with a suburban police department. Volunteered at local schools working with at-risk youth, kids who were just like I was, struggling to stay in school and out of the streets. That is why I am passionate about helping others. I wish I could say that every young person I've met took the advice I tried to give to help them turn their life around. The truth is some have, and some haven't. I can't keep up with everyone I meet, but I hope that something I've said stuck with them, and, at some point, help them to make better choices.

Since you decided to pick up this book, I don't believe you are one of those people.

I don't want to scare you, but I have to be real with you. Every decision you make or don't make has consequences. If you decide today that you don't want to learn and grow, hang with the wrong people, and not invest in yourself, your life will be hard. It will be hard for you to get a good job, start a business or get into colleges.

It will be hard for you to leave home and live independently. It will be hard for you to buy the clothes, cars, homes, and vacations that we all want. These are rewards that come from working hard—and smart—and making good choices.

If you want to live a successful life, you must make the right decisions now to move you in that direction. Listening and learning from people who can help you make better decisions, avoid mistakes, reach your goals, and recognize opportunities that you may not otherwise learn about is critical to your success. This is what knowledge is all about.

Deciding to be obsessive about acquiring knowledge is one of the most important choices I have ever made. When I decided to start listening to people who knew more than me, people who had been down the road I wanted to go down, people who had successfully done what I wanted to do, my entire life changed, for the better. When you open your mind, great things happen. All of those things that I mentioned that I've created in my life—the businesses, the investments, the career, then reaching back to help youth in my community, the success—wouldn't have been possible if I hadn't found people and other resources, primarily books, that could show me the way. The knowledge I have learned is the compass that guides my life and decisions. And since I follow it every day, I have created a life that is beyond anything I could have dreamed of as that knuckleheaded kid in the Chicago streets.

I want you to use this book as your own compass and Success GPS. This book will guide you on important decisions such as:

- Mapping out a vision for your life and defining what success looks like for you
- Setting goals to help you achieve your dreams
- Choosing a college and career
- Getting mentally and physically healthy
- Starting your own business
- Managing and saving money
- Investing so you can become financially free

Are you ready to create the life you want? Let's go!

How to Use This Book

To get the most from this book, follow this simple plan:

1. This book was designed as a reference guide. So, you can read it cover to cover, or you can use the table of contents to find the topic you are interested in learning about and focus on that.
2. Read each section/chapter once. Then read it again.
3. As you read, stop, and ask yourself how you can apply what you learned.
4. Underline and highlight sections that are important to you.
5. Get a new notebook that is dedicated to everything you need to write down as you work through the exercises.
6. Come back to this book every month (or as often as you need to) to refresh your memory.
7. Discuss your favorite topics with friends and family. You are a leader, and leaders teach others. When you learn something helpful, share it. That's how we all grow together.
8. Keep learning! Everything that I will share with you in these pages is just a starting point. There will be topics discussed in this book that you need more information on. Search the internet to learn more. There is a wealth of information at your fingertips to go beyond this book. Read articles from reliable sources. Find more books on the topic. Listen to podcasts from experts. Keep feeding your mind and applying the knowledge you find. You will be amazed at the results.

Section One

Decided Who You Want to Be

In high school, I never knew what I wanted my life to look like. I got up every day got dressed and went to school without a purpose. I never had a vision beyond high school, other than dating the hottest ladies. Nothing related to what I wanted after I walked across that stage at graduation. With no sense of direction, I could not lead myself or anyone else, so I was a follower. I wasn't living. I was just existing.

After stumbling through life well into my twenties with no sense of direction, I realized that I needed to take control of my life if I ever wanted to change it. I needed a vision. When I did that, everything changed. My life started to make sense. My attitude towards people and life in general changed for the better. I began achieving goals that I did not think were possible.

The first step in mapping out a vision for your life, and creating a guide to getting there, is asking yourself a simple question:

Who do you want to be?

Create a Vision for Your Life

When you close your eyes or daydream about your life in 20 years, what do you see? What college did you graduate from? What degrees or certifications do you have?

Are you working a 9 to 5, Where are you working? are you an executive at a big technology company? are you running your own business? Is your career creative or technical? Are you living in a home in the suburbs or a condo in the city? What kind of car are you driving? Are you on the beach sipping a Pina Colada with your family and friends?

Decide what you want for yourself and your relationships with others. Do you want a relationship that leads to marriage? Do you want kids? Do you want solid, supportive friendships that help you to grow and be a better person?

Think about what you want financially. How much money do you earn a year? Do you earn income solely from a job or from multiple sources? Are you financially supporting other people in your life, like your parents or siblings?

Last, but not least, decide what you want mentally, spiritually, and physically. This is important. How do you want to feel? Do you want a life that feels easy to manage, meaningful, and aligned with your purpose? Do you practice your spirituality? Is a healthy body important to you? Do you want to be in shape and have the freedom to go to the gym every day or several times a week? Do you want to have healthy meals prepared for you? How about a personal trainer who can come to your home or office? These are all health and lifestyle choices and essential aspects of your well-being and happiness. You want to be clear on what you need to feel good, inside, and out, so you can be the most positive and productive person possible.

When you know what healthy feels and looks like for you, you can set your life up in a way that helps you become that person.

Keep in mind that there are no right or wrong answers to any of these questions. This is your life and you can do and be whatever you want. Don't think about what is impossible or if the life you want to live feels out of reach. Because it is not. Nothing is off-limits. You have a big, long life ahead of you. Make it whatever you want.

I know it may be difficult to look so far into the future and think through all of these details, but it is necessary. Every successful person you know personally or who you admire had a clear, specific vision for their lives. Success is not something that happens by accident—it happens as a result of knowing exactly what you want out of life, setting goals (which we'll talk about next), and doing whatever is necessary to achieve those goals. This level of focus and commitment is what will set you apart from people who are just wandering through life. You are different. You are built differently. You think differently. You want more for yourself and your life. You have a vision.

Action Steps

Once you see the vision for your life and decide who you want to be, write it down.

1. Get your notebook.
2. Write out the full vision for your life. List every detail based on your answers to the questions above. Do not leave anything out.
3. Sit back and think about your future. As you read through your vision, you should feel excited about your dreams and the life you will create for yourself. If you don't, get rid of what doesn't feel right to you. Keep in mind that this is not about what anyone else has suggested or told you to do. This is your vision, your dreams, and what you want. Follow your own path.

You Can't Be What You Don't See

In addition to writing out your vision, I recommend a few things to help you to take your dreams from black and white to full color:

Create a vision board. A vision board really brings everything you want in life in a visual way. You can Google examples of vision boards to get an idea of what one looks like and how to put it together.

Gather some old magazines (you can ask your family, teachers, library, or bookstore's if there are any outdated copies around). Get a piece of large, white poster board, a pair of scissors, and one or two glue sticks from an arts and crafts store or a store that sells school supplies. Cut out words and pictures from the magazines that depict your life vision, and glue them to your poster board. When you are done, hang it on a wall or somewhere you can see every single day, ideally when you first get up in the morning. It will be a constant reminder for you to keep pushing.

Find inspiration online. As you are on the internet and social media, search for people who are living the life you want to live. Look for people who have the career or business you want. Pick up a magazine on the industry you are interested in and see who is featured in there. Find others who share the relationship and lifestyle you see yourself with. There may even be people in your county or city who have the life and career you want. Look around and see who you can find.

Discover those who work hard, grind, and hustle for what they want. These are your heroes, the people who you look up to. Once they are on your radar, you can watch how they move and follow suit. Study them for inspiration and information.

Talk to people. You will be surprised at how many people are willing to share information about how they became successful if you find the courage to ask. Use social media to reach out to your heroes. If you cannot find them that way, try email (you will be amazed at what a Google search can reveal). Ask them for 15-20 minutes of their time, either on the phone or in-person if you can.

Whenever you have a chance to get in front of someone important, remember their time is valuable. Be on time (in fact, be early if it's a face-to-face meeting), and come prepared with specific questions. Here are a few examples:

- What suggestions would you give me for (fill in the blank with a question related to what you need to know. It could be getting into a specific school, starting a career or business in a certain field, investing in real estate, etc.)
- What have been your biggest mistakes and what did you learn from them?

- Is there anyone else in the industry that you would suggest speaking with?
- Do you have any opportunities to intern or shadow you?
- Is there anything I may be able to help you with? (This is super important. When you are asking someone to mentor you or give you inside information, be willing to give them something in return.) *"Always give before you ask"*

We all need to see things to believe them. Keep your vision in front of you, by constantly seeking information, and surrounding yourself with images and relationships with people who are where you want to be.

Action Steps

1. Set aside sometime in the evening or a weekend to work on your vision board.
2. Once you find your heroes online, pull out your planning notebook and make a list of them. Try to find at least 5 people who inspire you.
3. Start reaching out to people that you want to interview.

Going from vision to plan

You have your vision. You know what you want. Now it is time to develop your plan to make it a reality. It's one thing to see something you want. It's something else to do the work to make it happen. But when you have a solid plan, that work becomes clearer and easier to execute.

When someone decides to start a business, one of their first steps is to create a business plan. This plan is a document that details everything about the company, including how the company is structured, what products or services it provides, how it is different from other companies who sell and do similar things. That is all useful information, but one of the most important aspects of any business plan is how the business owner intends to reach their goals for getting more customers and making more money. An effective business plan defines every step that an entrepreneur will take to reach their objectives.

Their vision for their business is simply a starting point. It means nothing without a clear strategy to make that vision happen.

Your life is no different from any business. As the CEO of your life, you need a plan too. A plan is what keeps you on track. Think of it like a checklist that lists out everything you need to be successful on your journey. I am certain there will be roadblocks but having a plan helps you to bounce back quicker.

Action Steps

1. Grab your notebook.
2. Look back over the vision you wrote out.

3. For everything you want, write out the steps it would take to get there, in order of how you need to do them.

For example, if your plan is to attend an Ivy League college, your first step is to start researching the colleges. Then, you will need apply for financial aid to pay for tuition, visit the schools, and find friends who are on the same path. (Remember, if you want to be the best, you must hang with the best.)

Let's say you want to open your own software development company. Your first step may be to become an expert in the type of technology you want to develop, either by going to college to get a degree, getting a certification, teaching yourself the skills, or maybe a combination of all of those. Then, you may want to find a mentor, write a business plan, create a team, and find clients to grow your business.

Remember, this is your checklist to be sure you stay on track to getting where you want to go. Every week, you should revisit the plan to ensure you are on the right track and make necessary adjustments.

Your plan will also save you time, energy, and ultimately money. If you want to become a nurse, you wouldn't attend a school that does not have a nursing program and you wouldn't waste time and money taking law classes. Every action you take should line up with your plan. If it doesn't, it's a distraction.

"If you are not where you want to be DO NOT QUIT, instead reinvent yourself and change your habits." Eric Thomas

The S.M.A.R.T Way to Plan

When it comes to creating a plan for your life and setting goals for yourself, you want to be as specific and clear as possible. This is how you set yourself up for success.

One of the most effective planning and goal-setting techniques is the S.M.A.R.T method. Using this system, you will be able to set goals that feel real and achievable to you.

Here is a quick guide to help you set your S.M.A.R.T Plan:

(S) Specific- What goal are you trying to accomplish?

(M) Measurable- How can you measure your success? How will you know you have accomplished this goal?

(A) Attainable- You want to be sure you set goals that you can reach? What will stretch you, but is still within your grasp?

(R) Realistic- Know yourself, your level of commitment, and what you are willing to put forth to achieve your goals. Don't set yourself up for failure with goals you don't truly believe you can reach.

(T) Time-bound- When do you want to achieve this goal? State the day, month, or year that you want to accomplish that goal.

Your S.M.A.R.T Plan is priceless. Once you develop your own plan, it dictates every decision you make. With clear goals, you can decide who to hang with and who not to hang with, what books to read, and what to study. You will know how to live every aspect of your life, from what time to wake up and what time to go to bed. Your time becomes a lot more valuable when you have goals. You cannot waste it.

When you have a plan, you can account for your time. Let's look at two people and how planning influences each of their daily lives, and ultimately, their goals.

Meet Sarah...

Sarah has goals but fails to write them down. She wants to be a psychologist and work with children who have been traumatized by abuse. She is very smart, but she lacks discipline.

She wakes up when she feels like it. She is late for class. She hangs with the wrong crowd. She is out past curfew hanging with her friends at the park drinking and smoking weed.

Sarah is free to do as she pleases because she has no direction. There is no plan for her to follow. Instead, she hangs with the popular crowd. She manages to graduate high school, but since she did not plan for college, she got stuck working a retail job that she hates. She tries taking classes online while she works, but it's too hard to do both. She gives up on school, keeps working, and telling herself she'll get to her dreams at some point.

Now, meet Johnny…

Johnny wants to be an accountant at one of the top law firms in Chicago. He wrote out his S.M.A.R.T plan to execute. He had his best friend become his accountability partner to keep him focused, and then he read books about successful accountants. He has some friends who would rather hang out than study, and while he may see them from time to time, he decides to spend most of his free time with friends who were on a positive track. He spent most of his time with them or studying.

Johnny attended a top college in Illinois to receive his undergraduate degree. While in college, he researched the company where he wanted to pursue an unpaid internship for the experience. He applied for the internship and got it.

Then he went back to school to earn his CPA (Certified Public Accountant) license.

After his internship, he was offered a full-time job with that company.

Do you see the difference a plan and goals make? Both Sarah and Johnny had a vision for their lives and the potential to make those visions a reality. But Sarah didn't get serious, committed, and invest the time to plan out her goals so she could clear direction. Johnny did. If he was not clear on what he needed to do, and he wasn't so persistent and focused, he could have decided to hang with the wrong crowd and waste time. He didn't, and now he's reaping the rewards of his hard work and effort.

Lesson You Need to Learn: Don't be like Sarah.

Action Steps

Now let's map out your S.M.A.R.T Plan.

1. Start with the end in mind. What are you trying to accomplish? When are you trying to get there?
2. Work backward. Now that you have identified your goal, how will you spend your time getting there? Identify books, courses, or seminars you plan to attend in that field.

3. Form a mastermind group. Invite and include people that you share the same vision with and brainstorm ideas with each other. Meet on a monthly basis.

Do something daily that moves you towards your goals. Refer your S.M.A.R.T plan every day as your roadmap. When your feet hit the floor every day, you should know exactly what you need to do to move you closer to your dreams. Let your goals be your guide.

Short vs. Long-Term Planning

If working towards a twenty-year version of yourself feels too overwhelming at first (and it probably will), think about your plan in terms of short-term and long-term goals. For each one of the milestones below, you should have an educational, career, relationship, and health goals. Plan each phase of your life out.

Action Steps

Ask yourself these questions and write out your responses:

1. Where do you see yourself in 1-3 years?
2. Where do you see yourself in 3-5 years?
3. Where do you see yourself in 10 years?
4. Where do you see yourself in 20 years? (This is the milestone we used to write out your vision earlier a few sections back.)

You Always Need Another Plan A

Plan A or Plan A? I know we all heard the saying "Have a Plan A and a Plan B." However, I like to say, have two Plan A's. If you strive for Plan A but cannot achieve it, this may have you feeling like a failure or incompetent. However, what if you had another Plan A? You will still feel successful. You can put the same effort and energy into your other plan, and still reach your ultimate goals.

Having a Plan B can seem like you settled for mediocrity when we know this is not the case. Having a plan B could be discouraging and lower your moral. However, Life happens, and situations will arise that are out of your control. You may not get accepted to the first college you apply to. Your family may decide that it's not wise for you to take on $136,000 in debt to attend a university out of state, so a state school or community college may be a better a fit. Your parents may get sick in your junior year, and you'll need to take time off from school which means pushing graduation out one year. These are all common scenarios that students like you work through every day. The ones who stick to their plans, rise above challenges, and get back on track are the ones who still win at the end.

From now on, have two Plan A's. Focus on getting across the finish line and winning; it's not important how you get there, what's important is that you made it.

Action Steps

1. Write out your other Plan A.
2. Take this plan through the S.M.A.R.T. planning steps from above.
3. Know when you need to pivot from your first Plan A to your second Plan A. Remember, good goals are time-bound, and you should have a deadline for each one. If you find that you're getting close to your deadline for a goal and you haven't achieved it yet, it could mean it's time to switch lanes and start another plan.

Success Requires Sacrifice

At any age, life should be fun. Anyone who tells you to just work without coming up for air and to enjoy life is being unrealistic. Taking time out for family, friends, and activities you enjoy should be factored into your overall plan. Fun is like fuel to keep you going. But you need to balance fun with your priorities.

There are a lot of opportunities for you to have fun now. But remember what you do now will affect the rest of your life. Sometimes, you will have to give up fun to focus on your goals. In order to get where you want to be, you have to be willing to pay the price. You have to be willing to make some sacrifices.

There will be times when you want to sleep, but you'll have to get up and get to class, stay up late to study, wake up early to jump start your day. You may want to hang out with friends and party, play video games or just chill and watch TV. But you can't. There will always be another party, the video games will be there, and the TV isn't going anywhere. Sacrifice now so you can live well later.

If you find that you are not making enough progress towards your goals, look at how you are spending your time. What are you doing between breaks, what are you doing over the summer, and even after school? We all make time for the easy things, but we run away from things that are difficult. Let's change our paradigm *TODAY!*

"Do what is easy and your life will be hard. Do what is hard and your life will become easy" Les Brown

Here are some questions to ask yourself:

- Is what you are doing every day moving towards your goal or away?

- Are you studying or hanging out?
- Are you staying up late reading or playing video games?
- Are you spending too much time with your boyfriend or girlfriend, or looking for one?
- Are you following the follower or are you being a leader?

Be honest with yourself. If you've fallen off a bit and lost focus, don't beat yourself up. But once you realize there is a problem, it's up to you to fix it. Reassess your goals, what knocked you off course, get back to it. Set aside time for friends and fun so you have something to look forward to. If you work hard Monday-Thursday, you can have Friday, Saturday, and Sundays to hang out. You can do it all—just not at the same time.

Every decision count, every minute counts. Do not waste your precious moments. Plan your life around your goals.

"If you are not willing to pay the price, you will never be able to see the reward."

Action Steps

Reflect on these questions:

1. What activities in my life are taking up a lot of my time, but are not moving me towards my goals?
2. What relationships are taking up a lot of my time and becoming a distraction?

3. How can I adjust my schedule to make room for the activities and relationships that are important to me?
4. What is my ideal schedule? What days and times do I need to set aside for each of my goals? What days and times do I need to set aside to relax and have fun?

Manage Your Time

As you are mapping out your plan and goals, you may be wondering how will it get done. Focus is important, and so are establishing priorities. Both are much easier when you master time management. Managing your time well is the key to success—from now until adulthood. The people who can focus the most, eliminate distractions and stay productive are the people who stay winning.

While 24 hours a day may seem like a lot, the reality is, it isn't. Once you subtract 6-7 hours a day for school and another 8 hours for sleep, the remaining 9 hours could literally fly by if you're not careful.

To make it easier to manage your time, write out a To-Do list every day.

Action Steps

1. Using your goals as a guide, write down the tasks you want to accomplish for the day.

2. As you go throughout your day, check off tasks as you get them done.

3. Your goal should always be to get through your To-Do List every day and be able to check off everything on your list.

I strongly suggest writing out your To-Do List every night before bed, so you know exactly what you need to accomplish the next day. I assure you, having this daily routine will set you up for success!

Don't Give Up. EVER.

Award-winning actor Denzel Washington has said, "without commitment, you will never start. Without consistency, you will never finish." Commitment is the core of everything you do—or don't do—in this life. You must want to achieve your vision and dreams for your life more than anything else around you. You must commit to it and refuse to allow anything or anyone to stand in your way.

You can never give up on yourself or your dreams, regardless of how hard it gets.

Giving up is the easy way out. Think about the successful people you read about. What if they had given up? If Martin Luther King had given up, we would not have the civil rights that we have today. If Steve Jobs had given up, we would not have Apple. If Oprah had given up, we would not have her network or her perspective on personal growth and spirituality. If the doctors, lawyers, inventors, and scientists who do amazing things every day had given up, we would not have the heart transplants, laws, or technology that we are benefiting from every second of every day.

What will the world miss out on if you give up? Think about that.

Life will get hard, and it will knock you down. Everyone had to overcome some hard experiences and so will you. You will feel like giving up and giving in. You will feel like letting your dreams die. But you can't give in. You will have to fight for the life you know you were meant to have. You will have to fight for your goals. You will have to fight for yourself.

If I had given gave up, I would not have been able to write this book. I failed the 6th grade, and when the time came to go on to middle school, I sadly watched all my friends go on while I had to repeat a whole year. The anger, frustration, and resentment I felt were unexplainable. I was also humiliated. Everyone knew I had failed. Kids laughed at me and teased me all summer. I lost friends. I lost confidence in myself. But I didn't lose who I was destined to be.

Yes, my mistake set me back a year, but it made me stronger mentally and emotionally. As a pre-teen, failing 6th grade was so hard for me. I contemplated taking my own life. It was so hard to fight the shame and embarrassment I felt. There weren't many people that I could turn to so that I could talk out my feelings and get some help. I didn't know if I should go back to school at all. I stopped dreaming, I felt lost and lonely with nowhere to go.

Fortunately, I found the courage to face my fear and failure and went back to repeat that year. I returned that summer with a new fire in me. I was focused and determined to never be in that situation again. I wasn't a perfect student, but I worked hard. I never failed a grade again. I wanted to be successful. So that's what I did. I didn't give up and neither should you.

If the work to achieve goals was easy, then everyone would do it. But the reality is, while we all can do it, there will always be people who won't. You are capable. You are someone who refuses to give up. **You will win.** The world is waiting for the gifts you are holding inside of you.

NEVER give up!

Action Step Bonus: Write a Letter to Your Future Self

Write about where you will be one year from now. Speak as if it has already happened. Include how you will feel when you receive your goals, and what rewards you will have as a result of your hard work.

For this first year, write about where you want to be in life. What school will you attend? What will your grade point average be? What kind of person will you be?

Mark in the calendar one year from the day you write this letter. Open the letter and see how far you came. Assess how much closer you are to your goals with these questions:

- Did you stay on target?
- Are you living where you want to live?
- Are you working where you want to work?
- Are you in the school you want to attend?
- Did you get off target?
- How far are you away from that future you?
- What do you need to adjust?

Be sure you align your plans with your dreams.
Utilize every moment.

Section Two

Choose the Right School

For many of the goals that you've laid out for yourself, education is a big part of your plan. Whether you are planning to enter the corporate or government world, start your own businesses or work in a more creative field as an artist or dancer. You will have to either obtain a degree or certification or study to learn more about your craft and perfect it at a professional level.

Before we move on, let's talk about a question that comes up often: *Do I really need more school after high school?*

There are some people who believe that it's impossible to start a career in anything without going to college. And some feel it's a waste of time and unnecessary. There are plenty of successful people, like Mark Zuckerberg, Bill Gates, and Russell Simmons who either dropped out of college or never set foot on campus as a student. I am sure you personally know someone who makes a lot of money and lives a good life who mastered a skill on their own, kept learning, and either got a job that allowed them to work their way up or became their own boss by becoming an entrepreneur.

If you are on the fence about college, the first question you need to ask yourself is: *Do I need college to do what I want to do?*

The truth is, you may not. Perhaps a technical or art school is the answer for you. Maybe you need a certification from an accredited organization, or online courses. Every industry has its own path.

Research is your friend. If you haven't done this already, Google the career you are interested in and find out what educational requirements are usually needed.

And do not forget your Plan A's. (Go back to the last chapter if you need a refresher). A degree may not be needed for your first Plan A, but maybe you need it for your second Plan A (the one that you'll put into play if your first option doesn't work out). Should you consider majoring in one field and minoring in another, so you have options? Something to think about.

Go back to your vision and explore your plan. Then explore all possibilities for reaching your goals. Choose the best path for you and make it a part of your S.M.A.R.T plan.

The sooner you're clear on what schools you'd like to apply to, the better. As a freshman in high school (if not before) you should be clear on what college or institution is best for you.

Deciding what school or institution is best for you depends on several factors.

- What are the admission requirements?
- What is the deadline for applications based on when I want to enroll?
- How much does the school/program cost?
- How will I pay for it? (We will talk about this later in the book).

The easiest way to find this information is to visit the school's website.

Action Steps

1. Make a list of the schools that interest you.
2. Visit each school's website. Go to the Admissions page to learn more about admission requirements, application deadlines and how to arrange campus visits so you can experience the school in person.
3. If you still have questions, contact the Admissions office to get answers to any additional questions you may have.

Get Those Grades

Every school has different admissions requirements. Some are looking for students who have volunteered a lot and done work in their communities. Others are focused on athletes, while others zone in on leadership. But those highlights are usually secondary to what colleges look at first, and that's your grades.

You may think grades don't carry a lot of weight, but they matter a lot. Almost any college you apply to will consider your grades when determining if you are a good fit for them. Not every college will expect you to have a 4.0, but they are looking for students who take their grades seriously. Before anyone has a chance to meet you, see your personality, and learn more about the value you will bring to their campus, your transcript is all they have to judge you on at first.

Your grades say a lot about you. An A student is assumed to be disciplined and focused, while a student with mostly Ds will be viewed as a slacker. We know that these assumptions are not always true, but when submitting an application package to a stranger, they don't have much to base a decision on. So, you want to keep your grades as high as possible.

At the beginning of each quarter, all students start with the same grade in each class, an A. When you show up to class late or don't show up at all, miss assignments, or fail to pay attention to what's expected of you, your grades  slip. Every grade affects your overall Grade Point Average or GPA. Each grade is worth a certain number of points. Your GPA is determined by dividing the total number of points earned by the number of credit hours attempted. It does not matter if the classes are remedial, regular, or advanced.

If your grades aren't great, and you're reading this book, you can turn them around, if you start now. Here are a few tips:

- ***Turn in all your assignments on time.*** They don't have to be perfect, but you have to give it your best.
- ***Get help.*** If you don't understand something, ask. Get a tutor or ask another student who is excelling in that subject for assistance. This gives you an opportunity to learn more and may even get you some face time with your crush if they are more familiar with a certain subject.
- ***Focus.*** Watch your grades like you monitor your likes on Facebook or Instagram. If your grade on a progress report is not what you expected, get with your teacher, and put an action plan in place to get that grade up before the end of the quarter.

In my sophomore year, my GPA dipped to 1.7. Talk about low! I remember opening my report card that quarter and feeling my heart sank to the floor. I knew I had been slacking off but seeing that number scared me. I knew I had to do better.

I worked diligently for two years to bring my GPA to a 3.0. It was not a 4.0, but I was still a far cry from where I started. It took 110% of constant determination, better study habits, and humbling myself to ask for help with my assignments. Once I got my grades up, I never let them slip again. I felt more confident applying for colleges, knowing that my GPA was at least average, which is all I needed to be considered for admissions. If I can do it, so can you.

Your grades can open doors—and they can also pay for college. As of 2018, the average cost of college tuition was approximately $34,000, for one year. That means you can expect to spend about $136,000 to walk across that stage with your degree. Some students are fortunate to have families who can afford to pay their way through school. But most students find themselves taking on student loans, or searching for other funding sources, such as scholarships and grants.

Action Steps

1. Set goals for your grades at the beginning of each school year. Decide what grade you want for each class and be clear on what you need to do to get it.
2. Assess where you are with your grades regularly. Keep track of them so that progress reports and report cards don't catch you off guard.
3. If you're struggling in a class, talk to your teacher and come up with an action plan. Get a tutor, makeup assignments or do extra credit—do whatever is necessary to get back on track.

Free Money: Finding Grants and Scholarships

Eligibility for grants and scholarships is typically based on three things—academic, athletic performance, and financial need. Competition for this "free" money is stiff. Therefore, your grades matter. The higher your GPA, the more options you have for scholarships that you may be eligible for.

As you are creating your plan to pay for college, there are lots of options for grants and scholarships to help. Here are a few options to consider:

- *Membership Organizations:* If your parents or a family member belong to a membership organization, such as Jack and Jill of America), they may have scholarships available. Fraternities and sororities often offer scholarships to local students as well.
- *Local Churches:* Churches in your community may offer scholarships to students.
- *Social Clubs:* Clubs such as Kiwanis International and Rotary International have chapters across the country that may offer scholarships.
- *Join a club:* Colleges love well-rounded students. In addition to playing sports, join organizations at your school. You can also look for clubs outside of school to participate in if there is something that interests you.

The more creative you are with finding funding for college, the more likely you are to find alternatives to student loans. Try to make student loans your last option. The interest is high and the monthly payments skyrocket once you graduate. The average student loan payment is $400 per month, and that is on the low end. A payment that low is barely covering the interest on the loan, which means you could be paying off student loan debt for the rest of your life. Take it from me, it's 2020 and I am still paying college debt from 2008 and I'm not close to being done.

Your goal is to keep your debt as low as possible so that you can have more disposable income to invest in your dreams, as opposed to having every dollar you earn allotted towards student loan payments and other bills. If you must borrow money for school, be smart about it. Research all your options, including careers that offer loan forgiveness, such as teaching in certain communities. (There is a lot of criteria with these opportunities, so understand it will not be easy), and community colleges and in-state universities where you can still get a great education at a much lower cost.

There are also some companies that will pay for your college if you intern with them or work for them after you graduate. You can also apply for work-study jobs.

Become a Resident Assistant and Live on Campus for Free

I had no idea what a Resident Assistant, or RA, was until after I finished college. But I wished I had known, especially once I found out this position could have covered my housing expenses!

A RA is an individual who is responsible for assisting younger students who live in the same residence hall. An RA normally applies for the position in their second year in college, after they have completed 40 hours of school. RAs are like mentors; they coordinate activities in the resident halls and ensure residents are connected, mediate issues, and ensure things run smoothly in the dorm. If you have ever watched reruns of the popular show "A Different World", characters like Jalessa Vinson and Whitley Gilbert were RAs in college. Sound like fun?

Well, maybe this will convince you: RAs get a financial stipend per semester, *free* housing, food, parking, and discounted tuition. Yes, I said *FREE*. This should be incentive enough for you to at least consider this.

As an RA, you will need to be a good problem solver and communicator. You will learn how to balance a job while working, build your network by bonding with other RAs and students, and save money. All of these are great reasons to become an RA or at least think about it.

When it comes to paying for college, know what options are available to you, and choose wisely.

The earlier you find out what grants, scholarships, funds, and special programs are available to you for college, the better. Don't wait until your senior year to start researching opportunities and figuring out your plan. Get started as soon as possible.

Action Steps

1. Visit https://studentaid.gov/
2. Google to find other grants and scholarships that you're interested in.
3. Go to https://studentaid.ed.gov/sa/fafsa to learn more about other federal student aid options, including loans, that are available to you. (Complete a Federal Application for Federal Student Aid FAFSA) after consulting with your parents about options.
4. Talk to your teachers and guidance counselors to find out about other grants, scholarships, and work-study programs that may be available to you.
5. Make a list of the programs that you intend to apply for. Include qualifications, application deadlines and other important information.
6. Work your plan to meet the requirements to apply.

Skills That Pay Bills (Sports)

If you like sports, consider playing throughout high school so you can apply for athletic scholarships.

There are the traditional sports, such as basketball, baseball, and football, and there are recruiters and scouts who will find you, and practically throw scholarships at you if you're a star player. If you're good at those sports, by all means, play them. Competition for scholarships in those sports is stiff, so keep that in mind.

You may also want to consider participating in sports that are less popular, such as swimming, golf, and archery that give you a competitive advantage. While other athletes are clamoring to get one of a handful of spots on the basketball team, hoping to get a chance to actually play a few times a season, you could be dominating in the pool or golf course. College recruiters pay just as much attention to athletes in these sports, and there are plenty of scholarships available, with a lot less competition. Every year, students all over the country are receiving free rides through college thanks to athletic scholarships.

If you have sports skills, use them to reduce the amount of student loans needed to finance your education.

Action Steps

1. If there is a sport you are interested in, but you are not currently playing, decide if you'd like to try it out through a school or community team.
2. Research scholarship opportunities for sports you are interested in or are planning to play to see what's available to you.
3. Be the best!

I am An Upper Classman, I Got This!

So, now that you have a few years of high school under your belt you think you got it all figured out? Guess again! You still have a lot of planning and studying to do. Your junior and senior year is not the time to relax and take it easy, even if you've done well for your first two years of high school. Colleges are evaluating you based on your entire high school career. If you haven't decided what career path you are going to take and what college would be best for you, now is the time to start. Before your junior year ends, you should know what colleges you are applying to and what programs are the best fit for the career you want to pursue. You want to hit the ground running in your senior year by visiting schools and applying for acceptance. There is no time to waste.

Action Steps

Revisit your plan for college and career. Go through the first two sections of this book if you need to. Those topics will help you map out a solid plan for your future and help you focus on what's important in your junior and senior year.

Who Is Your Mentor?

At some point in our life, we need a mentor. A mentor is someone who can guide us along our paths and offer advice that can help us make better decisions. A mentor offers us clear direction that ensures we are on the right track. Mentors can introduce us to people and places that we may not have known about or had access to. Mentors add value to lives in many ways.

For someone to qualify to be a good mentor for you, the key is that they've achieved whatever it is you are seeking to accomplish. A mentor is someone who has been where you want to be, in their lives or careers. Mentors are successful, financially, spiritually, and mentally. They are steps ahead of you in the game, and because of that, they can help you to avoid pitfalls and roadblocks, and accelerate your success.

You can have different mentors for different areas of your life. You may have a mentor for your career or business, who is an expert in your field. You may have a mentor in church, who is very spiritually connected and consistent in their faith practice. You may have another mentor who is an investor and who is financially savvy that can offer insight on how to handle your money. It is possible to find all these characteristics in one person too.

Mentorship is essential for success. You need guidance, insight, and support from more experienced people who can help you go further faster.

Action Steps

1. Make a list of people who you believe would be a good mentor for you.
2. Reach out to them and request a short meeting. You can do this over the phone or in-person.
3. At the meeting, explain that you are seeking a mentor and why. Explain what you would be hoping to achieve and why you believe this person would be ideal to help you. Be sure to guarantee them that you are willing to work and listen, and tell them why you are a good person to invest their valuable time in.

If you approach a potential mentor with humility and a promise of hard work, commitment, and consistency, chances are someone will see your potential and be willing to support you. Don't be afraid to ask.

Who Is Your Mentee?

As an upperclassman, you have a lot of decisions to make. You're also having the time of your life as your high school days are quickly coming to an end. But you should also seek ways to mentor those who are coming behind you. You've learned a lot over the years, and you have advice and wisdom that will be of value to someone who is where you were once. Find a mentee to share that with.

Whether you are formerly mentoring someone or not, remember that younger students are watching. Set a good example. Treat others with respect. If you see an underclassman being bullied, teased, intimidated or disrespected, stand up for them. You are a leader, and you have a responsibility to look out for those coming behind you.

Always pay it forward to the people behind you. If you are seeking a mentor, or already have one, be willing to do the same for others. look out for younger students in your school or sports team, volunteering at a Boys and Girls Club, or take the time to speak with a younger kid in the neighborhood who gravitates towards you because you share a similar past, take the time to help them.

Reaching back to help someone else is the price we pay for success. When you are willing to help others, more people will be inclined and inspired to help you. This is how the world works. The more you give, the more you receive.

Action Steps

Commit to finding at least one person to mentor. If you haven't come across anyone in school, church, or your sports team, ask a teacher or leader for suggestions.

Get Involved

If you have not already, now is the time to start getting involved in activities outside of the classroom. Not only will your college applications look better (schools love leaders and well-rounded students), but you will expose yourself to new people and ideas and create opportunities to give back to your school and community.

Join social clubs, be a part of the student government committee, try a new sport, learn a second language- do not settle for average. You are at the perfect age to leave your mark on the world and set examples for the people around you and the ones behind you. Stretch yourself. Reach higher. And always pay it forward.

A common trait of the wealthy is paying it forward. So, if you want to be rich, why not start by developing the right habits now? One of those habits is giving back. Giving back does not have to be monetary. It can be giving your time, resources, or knowledge. Whatever you choose to do, just give.

It's important to "Learn, earn and pass it on." Jim Rohn

Volunteering is very noble, and it can be extremely rewarding. Sharing your time and knowledge with someone or an organization can bring fulfillment to your life and others. Everyone feels good about helping someone else. It is what we were made to do.

Giving back is a reminder that we are far more fortunate than we realize. There are many unfortunate people who do not have the privileges that we are lucky to have. There are people right in your community who have not been able to go to school, to surf the Internet, or to learn to read. There are homeless, hungry, and without a winter coat or shoes—right around the corner from you. Think about that, then decide to do something about it.

Volunteer at homeless shelters, domestic violence shelters, retirement homes or non-profit organizations. Wherever you choose to give your time or donations, make sure you come with an open heart and empathy for others.

Action Steps

Research opportunities to give back to your community. Find a cause you are passionate about and find organizations that serve people who need help with what you desire to do. Tell your parent or teacher what your interests are. Someone will point you in the right direction.

What Options Do I Have Besides College?

I understand school is not for everyone, but learning is. You may be wondering if college is for you. Perhaps you have some

interests in a career that don't require a college degree, or you are already skilled at something and you're ready to master it and jump right into the workforce after high school

Here are some careers that do not require a college degree:

- Mechanic
- Barber
- Cosmetologist
- Life Coach
- Health and Wellness Coach If any of these careers interest you, research certification programs and trade schools online to learn more about how to enter these fields.

What About Going Into The Military?

The military allows you the opportunity to choose from a range of professions. In most branches of the military, you can be anything from a pilot to a doctor or nurse. There are members of the military who become mechanics, language, and communications specialists. The possibilities are endless.

In addition to gaining a successful career, leadership skills, and the honor of serving our beautiful country, the military offers several life benefits. Financially, military members are eligible for excellent home loan programs that may allow you to purchase a home without a down payment. There are credit unions that are exclusively for military members and their families, which will offer you lower interest rates on loans and credit cards, along with other benefits that are not available to the public.

Action Steps

You can research alternate careers, including the military, online. School guidance counselors are great resources for information, or you can reach out to someone in one of these fields to ask questions about qualifications and opportunities. Most branches of the military have local offices where you can go in and speak with a recruiter in person about opportunities.

What Makes You Happy?

Happiness varies from person to person. We all get to decide what makes us happy in life. For some of us, happiness means having a nice car and house. Others want a lot of money and a lot of friends to eat out, travel, and enjoy life with. For others, material things do not matter; all they really want is a loving family to come home to every day. None of these things are right or wrong. We get to choose what we want and what happiness looks and feels like.

Everybody can be happy in this life. Happiness is inside of you— you must bring it out.

Your happiness and what you want for your future is what should drive your decisions, particularly when it comes to your career. You have to be clear about what truly makes you happy and go for the life you want. When it comes to your career, here are some questions to think about:

- What would you do every day for free?
- What can you do for the rest of your life and be happy doing it every day?
- What steps can you actively take to get there?
- Who could help you along the way?

Answer these questions without worrying about what others will think, or what you've been told you should do with your life. Only you know, deep down inside, what will make you happy. Be brave enough to go after it.

I have been working since I was thirteen years old. I have always been great at earning money, but one of my biggest regrets as a kid was not finding a job that I loved, a job that did not feel like work. A job that I loved to go to that I enjoyed. I didn't find that happiness and fulfillment until years later when I joined the police force, which opened opportunities for me to work more with young people and the community. I started exploring entrepreneurship as a personal trainer and real estate investor. These are careers that I am passionate about. I realized that when we find passion, we find careers and jobs that we don't mind working hard at. We don't mind putting in the extra time and hours to learn more skills so we can be more efficient at what we do.

I wish I had known years ago that it was possible to find jobs that paid great money and satisfied my happiness. I don't want you to spend years investing your time and talent in any—career, school, relationships—that don't make you happy. Take this time now, while you have it, to create a life on your own terms. You have choices and a world that is wide open to you to do, and be, and have whatever you want. Don't waste it!

Action Steps

Write down what makes you happy and read it every day. This becomes your life mission statement or your WHY. Why is it important to you? Why is important enough for you to sacrifice sleep, time, friends, and money? Your WHY is the reason you are not distracted by money, bad influences, haters, and naysayers. You need a WHY more than you need anything else.

When you are willing to give up one thing to have something else, that is when you know your WHY is clear and the path you are on is right for you.

Once you have written out your WHY, read it every day to stay motivated and focused on why you need to get up and grind.

Section Three

Show Up as Your Best-Self

Let me be real with you and cut right to the chase.

I wish I could tell you that we lived in a world where the way you wore your hair did not matter. I wish I could tell you we lived in a world where the clothes you wear every day don't matter, either. Or your name or even the color of your skin. In an ideal world, in a "fair" world, none of these things would be a factor in whether or not you got the opportunity to interview for that high-paying job or lucrative contract if you're running your own business.

So, I hate to tell you. Every time an adult who cares about you has told you to think twice about that hair color, tattoo, tongue ring, or to pull your shirt down or your pants up, they were right. They were also right when they've told you that there will always be people who will see you as less than just because of your race or ethnicity. This is the reality of the world we live in. You need to still win.

Notice I said *still* win.

Yes, there will be times when you will hear a "no" that should have been a "yes." You will not get the opportunity on your first try, or at all, and you'll have to figure out an alternate path to success (remember your two Plan A's?).

You cannot control people who will discriminate against you due to your race, disability, religion, or any other aspect of your life. But you can do the work. You can show people based on how you show up, that you are serious about success and demand respect. You can always show up as the best possible version of yourself.

When you walk into a room, everything about you is being judged. The way you wear your hair. The way you dress. The way you speak. The way you show up on social media and online. All this matters.

I am not telling you to not be yourself. But I am telling you to be aware of how you will be perceived. It's not fair, but you cannot dress and speak in a professional environment in the same way you would when you're hanging out with your friends. One of the most important rules of life is that there is a time and place for everything. Never forget that. Choose what you do, what you wear, and what you say based on the time and place.

You don't want to be ruled out of an opportunity solely based on how you look or speak. Present yourself well. You are here to win. So, you have to show up like it.

How Are You Representing Yourself?

There is a popular saying, "Dress how you want to be addressed." How true is this for you? When you look in the mirror,  from head to toe, do you see the image of someone who is ready to win looking back at you? Does your image say you are a serious professional? Do you look like you care about yourself?

If you answered, "no," then now is the time to start working on improving your image. Let's start making changes.

You may still be a few years away from entering the work world and starting your career, but you will be interviewing for schools, internships, and other opportunities. If your image needs work, now is the time to get started.

Also, you never know who is watching you. You may not think you are a leader or an influencer of others, but you are. You may have younger brothers, sisters, and friends who are observing quietly. When you show up well, you are inspiring them to do the same. I understand you want to fit in and stay in style, but DARE to be different. You are a trendsetter; everything starts with you.

We are all influenced by others. If you are not sure how to adjust your style and image, think about someone you look up to and mimic them, or at least take some tips. How do they show up? In addition to how they look, what type of person were they? How is their character? If you are a guy, I will bet that your hero is a handsome guy who is physically fit, respectful, charming, giving, and loving. Or if you are a young lady, you probably admire a woman who is beautiful, carries herself well, commands respect, is successful, smart, and kind. These are all great goals to have.

No, I am not saying you must *be* them or be perfect. Always be you. But there is nothing wrong with having role models. We all need them.

If you do not have a parent or elder that you aspire to be like, then choose someone you trust. Choose a person that is successful, with good morals and values. Teenagers often listen to their friends and/or peers instead of people who have been where they're seeking to go or who have achieved the goals they're seeking to reach. Your peers are rarely in a position to be mentors. Your friends can give you advice and opinions, and it's okay to listen.

But always have at least one adult in your life who you admire and look up to. You need leaders in your life to become a leader.

People watch to get cues on how to treat you, based on how we show up, taking cues on how to treat us. This is true in school, in professional environments, and in public. This is also true for the opposite sex. Men and women are attracted to each other based on appearance. When you show up well, you will draw people who are attracted to you for the right reasons, and you will have better relationships and connections.

Gents: Does your appearance make a statement to the ladies you want to date? Are you sending the message that you are a man who is serious and successful, and you are looking for a woman who is on the same path?

You are a king who is looking for a queen, not someone to play games with. Show up neat and tight. Command respect everywhere you go.

Ladies: Does your appearance make the right statement to the men you want to date? Are you sending the message that you are a woman who demands respect, requires a serious, successful man, and won't settle for anything less?

You are a queen. You are royalty and should be treated that way. Show up everywhere as the woman you want to be seen as.

Action Steps

As you are thinking about your appearance and what may need to change, ask yourself these questions:

- How are representing yourself?
- Does your image demand professional respect?
- Are you dressed like a respectable person?
- How do people respond to you when they see you?

Once you have answered these questions honestly, get started with a list of things you'd like to work on and start making changes.

Ask a successful adult or friend you trust to help you. There is always someone who is willing to support you—just ask.

Attitude is Everything!

Showing up well is not just about clothes and looks. It's your attitude too.

Think of your attitude as cologne or perfume. If you have a pleasant, easy-going, likable attitude, you will find that more people will want to know you and more doors will open for you. A positive attitude attracts positive people. Happiness, confidence, and optimism are aromas that others want to inhale all day.

Similarly, a negative attitude stinks. It repels people. No one wants to be around someone who is rude, disrespectful, and constantly negative. Have you ever met someone who never has a good day and is always looking to fight someone or start some shhh... (you know the word I am thinking of here)? You may find their antics entertaining for a while, but eventually, the dark cloud of negativity that always seems to follow them starts to affect you, and you start putting more and more distance between you and that person. Their stinky attitude and behavior are too much for you to handle. You don't want to spend too much time with that person, and you definitely don't want to become like them.

Keep your attitude positive. Be the person people want to be around.

Action Steps

1. Do you have a negative attitude?
2. Is it caused by you, others, or both?
3. What are some of the things that irritate you? Can you do anything about them? If yes, do it. That could mean changing environments, friends, or having conversations with people in your life who anger or upset you, being honest about your feelings, and working it out if you want to maintain the relationship.
4. When you feel your attitude starting to shift towards the negative, what can you do about it to calm yourself down or get back to a peaceful mindset? Maybe it's taking some

slow, deep breaths, taking a walk, or listening to some music. Find ways to keep your attitude in check.

Invest in Yourself

Investing in yourself means taking every opportunity you can to learn, grow, and develop. Investing in yourself is anything that makes you better, mentally, or physically (more on that later in the book). But when it comes to your mental and education, you want to read books, attend seminars, and study. There is a wealth of information out there about anything you want to learn about. Learn as much as you can. Read as much as you can.

Do you know there are approximately 24 million people in America that are considered illiterate? Reading is imperative. If you choose a topic that you want to learn more about and you study it 3-4 times a week for one hour a day, in 5 years, you would be an expert on that topic. One hour of your day is a small price to pay for expertise. There are millions of dollars in knowledge. Get as much of it as you can.

Every time you get a haircut, or your hair done, buy a book to read. The last thing you want to be is all beauty or good looks and no brains. Let your inside match the outside.

Attending seminars, conferences, and workshops is a great way to expand your knowledge, learn up-to-date information on a specific subject and meet like-minded people. Most Seminars are often taught by experts.

If you can't find an event hosted by an expert on a topic you're interested in, you can create your own. Bring a group of people together once or twice a month to network and learn from each other. You can meet at a Starbucks, library or in a classroom after school. This will also give people an opportunity to learn, educate and empower each other in their personal lives. There is nothing more satisfying than receiving support from your peers and sharing knowledge.

The more you know, the more you can teach and share. The more you can teach and share knowledge, the more valuable you are.

Successful people bring value to the workplace, their homes, and their relationships. People are paid for what value they bring to the table, and to solve problems. Problem solvers are always great additions to any team.

Action Steps

1. Find some topics that you are interested in learning more about.
2. Go to Amazon.com and search for books on that topic. Read reviews to see what others had to say about them. Choose one to start with.

3. Check your local or school library to see if they have the book before you spend money on it.
4. Once you have the book, set a goal to read at least 10 pages a day until you are done.
5. Get another book and keep reading!

Be Helpful

To be interesting, you must be interested. This means every conversation or relationship is not about you. Instead, you share the spotlight and look for ways to support others and help them to reach their goals.

You will be surprised at how many people have one-track minds. They are primarily focused on themselves. Those are the people who ask, "What can you do for me?" when the real question should be, "What can I do for you?" This is service. This is what God created you for, first and foremost—to be a servant to others.

We do not have to be in a customer service role to be a servant to others. We can all look out for others. Look for ways to bless people every day. It can be a text message to a friend expressing your gratitude for the friendship, treating your parents to dinner, paying for someone's food at a restaurant, writing your teacher an appreciation letter or giving them a card. These are called random acts of kindness. Do something daily to put a smile on someone's face. In your free time, consider volunteering in your community at a shelter for teens or find a group where you can mentor or tutor. Not only will you gain community service hours for school (*activities like this look great on college applications*) but you will be helping someone who needs you. The more people you help, the more people want to help you. Be kind.

Action Steps

Make it a point to do something kind for someone at least once a day. Preferably a stranger. This act of kindness will push others to do the same.

Section Four

Get Your Mind Right

As you are working on yourself, and becoming the person you really want to be, your mindset is so important. We have talked about how to set goals and how to increase your chances of success. But your mindset is key.

What you think about yourself determines what you can and will become. What you think about your future determines what it will be. The mind is an incredibly powerful tool. A positive mind creates positive actions. The flip side of that is if you think you are a failure, then you are. But if you think you are successful, then you will be.

Therefore, it's so important to prime your mind for optimistic thoughts, and to be your biggest supporter. Know that you are valuable. Push yourself. Remind yourself of what you are capable of, and everything that you must give to this world.

If you know that your mindset needs some work and you need to increase your self-motivation, do not worry. This section will help you get there.

Be Your Own Hero

A hero is a person who is idealized for their outstanding achievements, qualities, selflessness, and much more. When you think of a hero, who comes to mind? I am sure you can think of at least one person, and probably a lot more. We should all have people who we look up to and admire.

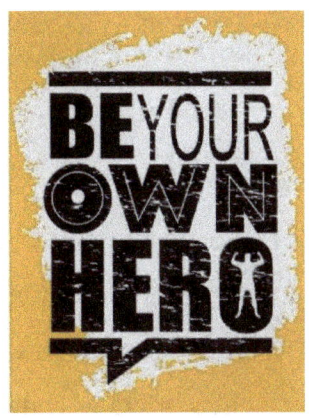

But starting today, I want you to add a new hero to your list. The person you see in the mirror every day. *YOU.*

I like to define heroes a little differently than someone who is known for their bravery. That is important, but I believe in heroes that are all around us, like you. heroes are:

- **H**onest
- **E**mpathetic
- **R**espectful
- **O**pen-minded

This is a HERO.

I know you can say that you are each one of those characteristics. You are a HERO, every day of every week. Give yourself credit for that. Put yourself on a pedestal and admire what a great person you are. Recognize yourself for all the work you are putting in towards your goals and your dreams. You have been through a lot, you have struggled, and you're still pushing through. You are a HERO.

We are all guilty of idolizing someone else, people who we think are more successful and who have done or are doing greater things. This is easy to do when we don't know that person's story. They have struggles and hard days, just like you. They are sacrificing something, just like you. They are committed to their success, just like you. They have a story and so do you. Be the HERO of your own story. Stay committed and consistent, and I promise, your time will come.

Just be *YOU!*

Action Steps

1. In what ways do you show honesty?
2. In what ways are you empathic to others?
3. In what ways are you respectful?

4. What is something you've had to open your mind about? How did that make you a better person?

Morning Motivation

One of the most important practices to develop a positive mindset is a morning ritual. Your mornings set the tone for your entire day, so you want your first thoughts and actions to be happy, peaceful, powerful, and make you feel strong and ready to win. You want a clear mind, free of yesterday's troubles and focused on the new day ahead, a new chance to work towards your goals and success. You want to feel energized and motivated. You can do this by creating a morning ritual for yourself—a set of things that you do every morning before you do anything else.

When you wake up, you want to find balance and relax your mind. Try to start your day without checking your cell phone, emails, or social media until you have finished your ritual. No matter where you live, create a quiet room free from distractions, especially electronic devices.

In your quiet space, your ritual can include anything you want it to. You may want to pray, writing out your thoughts, drawing, read something inspirational, or listen to some soft music or nature sounds. What you do is up to you.

My personal morning ritual includes affirming myself, practicing gratitude, and meditation. If you aren't sure where, to begin with, your own ritual, start with these three things. I am positive each of them will make a big difference in your day and your life.

I will talk about each practice more below.

Action Steps

Before we move on, you need to find your quiet space. It could be a corner of your room, or somewhere else in your home. Make sure your space is as clean and clutter-free as possible. This will set the right tone for your morning.

Affirming Yourself

I am a big believer in affirmations—words that you say to yourself to inspire yourself. Pumping yourself up and reminding yourself how great you are is incredible for your mental health and for  maintaining a positive outlook and attitude. As a part of your morning ritual, wake up every day and praise yourself.

Every morning, I practice The Power of I AM. I repeat statements to myself such as, "I AM smart, I AM healthy, I AM happy."

These are emotions that I want to claim and declare over my life. I say them over and over like I am chanting. When I say these words, I am sending a signal to my mind that I am all these things.

Try this and the same will happen for you.

Action Steps

1. Choose your I AM affirmations that you will say to yourself each day.
2. Write them down in your notebook.
3. Say them to yourself every day during your morning ritual.
4. You can also write them on Post-It notes or small pieces of paper and tape them to your bathroom mirror and recite them as you are preparing for school.

Practice Gratitude

Another great practice to include in your morning ritual is gratitude. When you wake up being thankful, it humbles you. In turn, it decreases anger issues, anxiety, aggression, and an argumentative frame of mind.

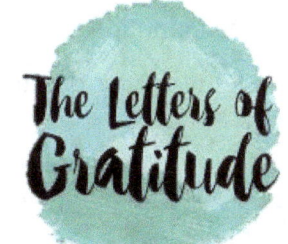

Think about everything you are grateful for. Be thankful for the people who love and care about you, family, friends, and opportunities. Be thankful to see another day.

These are important habits. Sometimes we do not realize the small things that are blessing in our lives, and that we take for granted, such as clean drinking water, clothes, food, being able to go to school and pursue any career path we choose. We are healthy and alive, that is something to be grateful for.

Giving thanks for all that we have is a way to keep our minds in a peaceful state, and to stay focused on the positive aspects of life.

Action Steps

The best way to practice gratitude is to list out everything you are thankful for. Write a list of things you are grateful for. List them every morning, and again at night if you had a bad day this will help you release the negative energy and focus on the positive.

Meditation for the mind

One of the most powerful practices to add to your morning is meditation. Meditation quiets the mind and relieves stress. Our day-to-day lives can create so much stress on our minds and bodies, more than most of us realize.

> Dream big. work hard. stay focused & surround yourself with good people.

Meditation can help us to get a handle on our emotions before we start our hectic days.

Start with practicing deep breathing. Controlling your breathing helps to quiet and focus your mind and helps to calm you down in stressful situations. Think about that time your teacher or parent got on your nerves. Sit in a quiet space. Close your eyes and breathe slowly, while counting to 10. *Breathe in through your nose out through your mouth.* Do these repeatedly until the stress is released. Breathing works wonders. So, before you decide to verbally attack someone, walk away, and practice your deep breathing. You will find that this exercise will get you back to a peaceful place.

If the idea of meditating sounds like a crazy idea, I challenge you to try it every day for one week. Notice how your frame of mind changes and how much calmer you feel. You can meditate any time of day, whenever you feel the need to relax.

Action Steps

Meditating on your own may be hard at first. If you cannot quiet your mind with just breathing, look up "guided meditations" on YouTube. These are pre-recorded meditation sessions where someone talks you through each step, telling you when to breathe and helping you to control your thoughts. Guided meditations are a great way to start getting into the practice.

Guard Your Mind

Your mindset is influenced heavily by what you hear and see. It may seem like you are just listening to a song on the radio or watching a television show, but if that song or show is filled with angry words, cursing, or other negative ideas and images, your mind is taking all of that in, whether you realize it or not. Your mindset and your behavior could be affected and that's not a good thing.

Of course, I'm not saying everything you listen to or watch is bad. But I am saying you should be mindful, especially when you are constantly listening to certain types of music, such as "crunk" or "drill" music. Listening to music like this all the time will put your mind in an aggressive state.

Have you ever noticed that you feel more hostile when you listen to certain songs? Imagine if you get up in the morning to drive to school, and you are listening to drill music all the way there. You are driving faster, swerving around cars, honking at people aggressively. This is road rage, and you can find yourself in an accident or being pulled over for speeding. I know you may be thinking this sounds far-fetched and couldn't happen to you. But believe me, it can. You would be surprised at how easily scenarios like this can happen when your mind is being subconsciously pumped with aggression.

If you usually go hard in the mornings with your music, try listening to something inspirational for the first hour of the day. No, it does not have to be gospel, but it must be something that puts your mind in a better place in the morning.

The news is something else to be mindful of, especially in the morning. The news offers some helpful information. But it can be more discouraging and negative than positive. With a constant stream of murders, robberies, and car accidents, along with bombings, wars, racism, and political battles, how can we expect anyone to feel upbeat if this is the first thing they hear?

It's okay to watch the news before work or school to see the weather or check the traffic on your route but ignore the negative things.

This goes for the internet and social media too. Online can be filled with negativity. So be careful.

There are also times when you must guard your mind against people, such as family and friends. We all have at least one negative person in our lives. Negative people like to gossip. They don't have anything positive to offer the conversation or the group. These types of people are always in some sort of trouble, complaining, or always looking at the glass half empty. Sure, everyone has problems. But for some people, their problems never go away, and they really aren't working to solve them. Negative people are like a dark cloud. When they come around, everything feels gloomy. When they leave, it's sunny again. Negative people are content right where they are. And sometimes, you must leave them there. We can choose when to hang with people like this and when to keep them at a distance. Always limit your time spent with negative people. They will bring you down.

Have you ever heard the old saying, "Birds of a feather flock together"? It's true. Negative people like to hang around other negative people, just like positive people tend to flock together. Think about it—have you ever seen an eagle playing around or eating with chickens or pigeons? You haven't? Me either. I am sure it is because eagles do not surround themselves with birds who are not on their level. Chickens and pigeons do not fly high or soar as eagles do. They stay local and make a lot of noise (gossip). Do not be a pigeon, you are better than that. Be an eagle and find other eagles to soar with.

Your mind is powerful, so be careful what you feed it. Choose wisely what you hear, what you see, and who you spend time with.

Your decisions will make all the difference in your day and in your future.

Action Steps

Take a few minutes to think about these questions:
1. What are you listening to every day?
2. Who are you listening to every day?
3. What are you watching regularly?

If you need to clean up what you are feeding your mind, start now. Do a mindset audit, and try to slowly ease out negative music, other media, and people.

Action Steps Bonus: Practice Mirror Affirmations

Before you leave the house, praise yourself. Look in the mirror and say, "Good morning, beautiful" or "Good morning, handsome." This may seem silly but keep practicing until you get used to it.

In addition to your morning rituals, these affirmations set the stage for the day ahead. Besides, you can't expect people to see something in you that you can't see in yourself. And you don't want to be dependent on the affirmations of others. You are royalty, so speak to yourself that way.

Section Five

Keep Your Emotions in Check

Anger Management: A Quick Lesson

Let us talk about emotions for a minute, particularly anger. In life, you will constantly run into people who upset you. There will be people who test you. And you will want to clap back. Sometimes you want to take it a step further and put hands on them. Think before you act. Always weigh the options: will this matter 5 minutes, 5 months, or 5 years from now? If the answer is "no" to all three, leave it alone. The angrier we are, the less clear our heads are. Learn to step back from situations and think through your actions, and the consequences, before you act.

But if you encounter a situation or a person that threatens you or your safety get help immediately. Never take matters into your own hands, if you feel uneasy about someone or about what someone said to you, find an adult to help you determine how to handle the situation. Leave this to mentors, parents, teachers, or police officers. Anyone who you feel comfortable talking to, preferably a professional who has the knowledge and experience to assist with your concerns. You need someone who can see the problem from an unbiased point of view and discuss the situation calmly with you.

Explain the situation to them. They will guide you on what to do next. That person may be willing to mediate and meet with you and the individual you are having a conflict with to help resolve the conflict. They will help you find a solution. **Do not** try to resolve big problems on your own. Get help.

What happens when you try to handle situations by yourself? Usually nothing positive.

Let us pretend you have heard a group of people talking negatively behind your back. They are gossiping about you and spreading rumors. Word gets back to you and you are angry.

Your first instinct would be to approach the person or group. But what if that group retaliates by jumping you? You get mad and *want* to get back at them, so you get your friends, your crew, and a brawl ensues and someone gets hurt. At this point, you could potentially be charged criminally for mob action, battery, and much more. You see how one decision could cost you time in jail, money, *or both*? Never make choices when you are mad.

I am speaking from experience. In high school, during our senior year, a friend and I found out that a group of students didn't like us, and they let it be known. Word got to us that they planned to fight us and some other friends after school. We got heated, and, instead of backing down, we showed up. It turned out to be more than a fight—it was a brawl of about 5-10 people. The teachers and administrators who eventually broke it up found out that I was defending myself, and while I got suspended for five days, it could have been worse. That situation could have cost me my graduation, time in jail, money, and hospital bills had I been hurt.

I could have avoided the suspension or even the entire situation if I had calmed down, took a deep breath and gone to a teacher to discuss the situation. Mediation could have been arranged between both sides to resolve the problems.

To some, this may seem scary or a snitch move, but it really shows who is the bigger person. We must be mature, even when no one else is.

What separates adults from children is the decisions we make under pressure.

Action Steps

Know your anger management plan. If you find yourself in a situation, know what techniques you can use to quickly calm yourself down and what adult or person of authority you can talk to when you find yourself in a situation. ***Remember, do not make decisions out of anger.*** Take a step back, collect your thoughts, cool down, and figure out what to do next.

Don't Sweat the Small Things

Anger is one of those sneaky emotions that can be hard to control. People upset us and life throws us curveballs. We must learn how to manage anger, sadness, disappointment, and embarrassment, knowing what deserves a reaction and what does not.

We often spend major time and energy on minor things. Although we are all different and we categorize a crisis differently, it is important to focus your energy on positive things. Keep things in perspective. Take a step back and assess if the situation is minor, and if you should breathe, cool down, and let it pass, or if you need to respond in a more serious way.

Here are some common scenarios that you may run into often:

Minor situations:

- A friend is talking about you behind your back.
- A relationship break-up.
- You missed the bus.
- You didn't get the latest shoes.

- You got a stain on your new shoes before you made it to school.

Major situations:

- You have a death in the family.
- You suffer a traumatic experience (i.e. car accident, victim to violence).
- You are without shelter or food.
- Your parents get a divorce.

A few things to consider about a major and minor crisis: As I stated earlier, we categorize a crisis differently. What is a big deal to you, may not be a big deal to me, and vice versa. You have a right to be upset about things that happen to you, whether they are minor or major. I only ask that you look at the bigger picture. Some people are without food and water, fighting to survive, have lost someone they love to violence or are battling depression and suicidal thoughts. When you think about those situations, someone talking about you behind your back is not that important.

Focus on your solutions—not problems. Know the difference between something that should knock you off your game versus something minor that you should let pass.

Life is a series of experiences. There will be good and bad days. Good relationships and bad ones. Happiness and disappointment.

Learn to process and navigate emotions. Ask for help and advice from adults you can trust. And know that above all else, you will survive—everything.

"A mark of honor is avoiding a fight not winning a fight"

Action Steps

1. Think about a situation in your life that is bothering you the most or have bothered you recently.
2. Are they minor or major situations?
3. How are you handling your emotions? Are these situations affecting your sleep, ability to focus, or attitude?
4. If so, find someone (an adult, a counselor, or someone you can trust) to give you advice and help you work through the situation.

Bullying is Never Tolerated

Putting your hands on anyone is never acceptable. The one exception to that rule is self-defense, which I don't need to dive deep into. I will say, use your judgment. You know when you are in a situation when you are in immediate danger and you're being physically attacked, as opposed to resorting to violence when someone upsets

you or says something you don't like. You know the difference. Guide your actions accordingly. Think before you act, always.

But let's talk about the violence that happens every day in schools, particularly bullying. Maybe you have been bullied, or you have bullied others in some way. Neither is okay.

Let us talk about what bullying is, so we are clear.

Bullying is the use of force, threat, or coercion to abuse or intimidate. Bullying can be physical, verbal, or online (formerly known as cyberbullying). Here are the common types of bullying:

Physical bullying is the most common form of bullying. This includes pushing, shoving, kicking, hitting, and punching. In many cases, the bully is bigger, stronger, and more aggressive than their peers.

Domestic violence is also a form of bullying. Domestic violence is the abuse of a family member, significant other or a roommate who lives in your home.

Verbal bullying is quite common. Bullies use this tactic of name-calling and insults to belittle their victims. Most of the time, verbal bullies target their victims when adults or people who are stronger than they are not around, knowing that if their behavior is caught, they will be stopped or punished.

Relational Aggression is emotional bullying. It happens when you are purposely isolated from groups and conversations. It's also common for bullies to start rumors to sabotage someone else's social standing.

Sexual Bullying is harassing a person because of their gender or sexual orientation.

Get familiar with these types of bullying so you will know them when you experience them or see them. Bullying is never okay and should never be tolerated.

Action Steps

It can be hard to identify bullying when you experience it. So, here are two questions to ask yourself in a situation, either physically or online:

- Do you feel an unwelcomed advance towards you?
- Do you feel threatened?
- Do you feel as if you are being forced to do something, and there will be repercussions if you don't?
- Have you ever felt less than after someone has made a comment to you or touched you?

If you are being bullied:

1. Tell the person to stop.

2. If they continue with the behavior, tell an adult or a person in authority (such as a teacher or administrator in school, a manager if this is in a professional environment or the police, depending on the nature of the situation).
3. Stop all communication with the person immediately. If the incident occurred on social media or online, block that person.
4. Record all contact and communication for evidence.

Never allow anyone to make you feel uncomfortable or threatened in any way. ***Nobody deserves to feel belittled. Do not tolerate that behavior towards you or anyone else***. When you see someone, who is being bullied or is a bully, be brave enough to say something or tell someone. You never know whose life you could be saving or changing. (National Centre Against Bullying , n.d.)

Section Six

Value Your Relationships

An important aspect of your life is people and relationships. None of us can live life alone, and we all need love and support from people around us. Relationships are about give and take—and appreciation. When we show people how much we value them and what they do for us, it makes them feel appreciated.

No one wants to be taken for granted. Always keep in mind how you want to feel in your relationships, and what you expect from others. I am sure appreciation is on that list, along with respect, kindness, and love. If you want these things, give them. (Guys, this includes you. Men should show love to the people who love them back too.) Your relationships will be healthier and happier when you value them, in every way.

Respect Your Elders

If you have elders around you, such as parents, grandparents, aunts, and uncles, you are fortunate. There are lots of kids in the world who have lost older family members, or never knew them at all. So be grateful for the family you have.

The great thing about parents and elders is that they have been places that you want to go. They have lived longer, and they have learned many lessons in their lifetimes. You may not always agree with their advice, but keep in mind that they have wisdom, and can often see way ahead of you. They have also known you for a long time, so they have love for you and want to protect you as much as possible. Before you tune your elders out, listen. This goes for your family and other adults, such as teachers and coaches etc. Think of them as mentors.

Always listen and respect them—.

When you respect adults, especially your parents, you are honoring their sacrifices. Parents give up a lot to raise you and provide for you. There are plenty of things they don't have so that you can have. Most parents want to provide a better life for you than they had. They want to prepare you for the real world, and for the day when you must take care of yourself. The same goes for teachers, counselors, and coaches. Those individuals may not put a roof over your head or buy your sneakers, but they care about you. All the adults in your life deserve respect. You don't have to agree with or like everything they say, but you have to respect it and be obedient. No talking back, no questions asked.

Remember, your attitude is everything!

"Your attitude determines your altitude." Zig Ziglar

Action Steps

If you know that your attitude has been negative or you have been disrespectful to an adult, apologize for it. It takes a mature person to say, "I'm sorry," especially when you don't necessarily feel like you were wrong. You can disagree with someone without being angry or disrespectful. If you got out of line with your Mom, Dad, or someone else, make it right with an apology and talk it out. You never know when it's their last day on earth.

Respect Your Friends

Respect should be the basis of any relationship, including friends. Respecting friends means being honest, treating them well (think about how you want to be treated), and not allowing anyone to disrespect them—including you.

One of the biggest forms of disrespect is to call someone out of their name. I know it's common to hear people playfully calling each other names (you know those five-letter ones that you can't say in front of your parents or pastor) that have become a normal part of music and culture. Those names are derogatory and disrespectful. Throw them out of your vocabulary.

If you are unsure if a name that you call your friend is disrespectful or offensive, ask yourself: What if someone I did not know call my family or friend this? How would that make me feel? That would not be cool, right?

There's your answer.

Lead by example. We earn admiration from respecting others. If you care about someone, do not disrespect them, or allow anyone else to do the same. Treat others how you would want someone to treat you.

Action Steps

Be more aware of how you treat your friends. Watch the words you say and how you joke and play with them. Be more mindful of their feelings.

A helpful exercise is to ask each of your friends how they feel about you. Ask how you can be a better friend. Listen openly, without getting defensive or upset. Learn from the conversations and grow.

The Crowd You Keep

One of the greatest motivational speakers in the world, Les Brown, once said, *People inspire you or they drain you* - pick them wisely." These are true words, and sound advice that you should use to decide who gets to be a friend, and who doesn't.

Your relationships will either make you or break you, and there is no such thing as a neutral relationship. People either inspire you to greatness or pull you down in the gutter. It's that simple. The people we associate with and spend time with will determine our future. We can follow friends down the right road or the wrong road. The choice is up to us.

Let's say, for example, you have two friends that are gang members. If you are spending a significant amount of time with them, the possibility of you falling into gang culture and becoming a part of that same gang is very likely. It doesn't matter how good of a person you are. It doesn't matter if you think you can dabble in their behavior and go home (trust me, you can't). It doesn't matter if you're a great student headed for college. If you decide that this is your crew, then you are accepting the consequences of being friends with people who can get you in serious trouble. Hanging with a known gang crowd could cost your life, someone else's life, or lead you to jail for years.

You may be thinking, "I am a teenager. How could I go to jail for a long time?" You can. Depending on the crime, you could find yourself in the juvenile justice system until you are eighteen years old and transferred to the adult jail. Say goodbye to your dreams, along with your family, friends and loved ones.

Jail is no place for someone like you! You *are* highly intelligent. Put your smarts and common sense to good use and stay away from people who are not headed in the same direction as you.

The scenario of gangs and jail time may seem extreme, but it happens every day. For some people, bad decisions don't always result in a ten-year jail sentence or losing their lives, but there are still consequences.

As a kid, I got caught up following the wrong friend, and it cost me dearly. I thought the guy was cool, and we were two knuckleheads, hanging out together. One day, we wanted to get on the train without paying. He decided to jump the turnstile, and I followed. As he ran, an officer caught me. I got arrested and he got away. It was a long embarrassing walk to the police station. Of course, he was at home relaxing while I was sitting on a cold bench waiting to be fingerprinted and put in the juvenile system. I knew better. But a lapse in judgment and deciding to be a follower instead of a leader who thought for himself, cost me a lot. If I had used my head, I could have avoided a mess, including embarrassing my family and a police record.

Now let's look at a positive example. Staying in the company of friends who are doing the right things in life will inspire you to do the same. If you hang with people who share the same passions as you, the ones who wake up early, get to school on time, and stay up late studying, you all will influence each other in a positive way. Instead of going to jail, you will be going to college. You can follow these friends into great careers and opportunities. Remember how we talked about birds of a feather flocking together? How eagles like to soar with other eagles? That is the benefit of keeping friends who are determined to succeed. If they fly high, they will take you too, and you'll do the same. Positive relationships are mutually beneficial. Groups of positive friends who can help each other are called your network.

Your network is the people you hang with, talk to, and associate with most. These could be classmates, friends, associates, and family. It is imperative to always maintain a solid network; it will determine your net worth. Networks open doors and create new relationships. It's not always about being "hooked up", but networks are about connecting you with the right people at the right time. If you are prepared, who you know can make all of the difference in the world for your life.

> *"Networking is not just what others can do for you; networking is what you can do for others."*

Build the right networks. Connect with people who are on the same path as you, people who you can help and who can, in turn, help you. Share your goals with those friends who get it and will motivate you to keep climbing—and stop wasting time with those who don't.

Action Steps

It may be tough to do, but now is the time to purge some friends if you need to. You know who is beneficial to you and who isn't. You are at a critical stage in your life. The decisions that you make now, the relationships you have (or do not have) will impact the rest of your life.

> *"No one fails alone, and no one succeeds alone." Eric Thomas*

Look around you. Who are you spending the most time with? Are these people positive or negative for you? If they are negative, you must start limiting your time with them or cut the relationship completely.

The Person with No Goals

A person with no goals has no direction and is easily influenced by others. Having no direction will lead you down the path of being a follower – not a leader. We were all created differently with unique attributes. As individuals, we all bring something different into this world. Know what your value is, and what you must contribute to the world. When you know who you are and how great you are, you are less susceptible to people whose lives are not on the same positive path as yours.

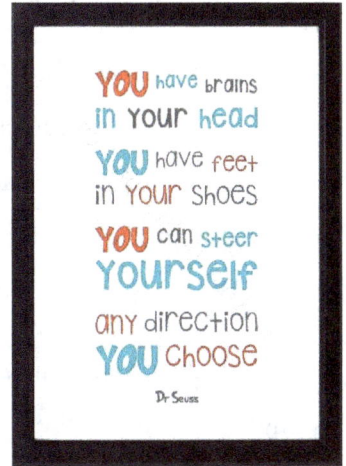

Set goals for yourself, and at the top of that list is to never be a follower. You have your own mind and your own ideas for your future. You know what you want out of life. You don't need to copy or follow anyone else. You are unique, and that is what makes you exceptional.

Besides, if you are too busy being someone else, then who will be you?

Action Steps

Here are some questions to ask yourself:

1. What am I bringing into this world?
2. What is unique about me?
3. Why am I valuable?
4. Am I following someone else's vision for my life? Or am I living true to who I am?

Get clear on your value, your goals, and who you are. Set your bar high, and watch others follow you.

Let's Talk About Dating

At some point in your life, you will be dating. You may have a girlfriend or boyfriend in your life now, a significant other that you love and enjoy spending time with. Or you may be waiting for the right person to come into your life. When we think about love and dating, we often think about what we're looking for in someone else. That is important. We want people who are kind, respectful, loving, supportive, and who can help us to achieve our goals in life. But to attract someone like that, we have to be that person.

When it comes to dating, there are some things that we should say or do to show kindness and respect. Some of these are small, but these gestures and behaviors mean a lot.

Let's talk about some of the important things to keep in mind when it comes to dating.

Gents:

Okay, guys. Listen up. For women, manners and chivalry are very important. Women always want to feel protected and respected, period. Here are some things you should always, always do for a lady:

- Open the car door for her and close it once she is seated inside.
- Walk side-by-side with her, but always stay near curb while your woman walks on the other side. This shows that you are there to protect her.
- Hold the door for her when you go into a building.
- Help her with her coat.
- When you take her out to eat, pull out her chair before she sits.
- Hold her hand and look into her eyes. When talking with her, give her your undivided attention.
- NEVER let your eyes wander to look at another woman when you are with your girl. I don't care how beautiful she may be. Show your lady the respect she deserves.
- If you invite someone on a date, you should expect to pay. Although men generally pay for dates, there are some situations where a woman may want to pay for the date or even split the bill. But the general rule is whoever extends

the invite should be prepared to pay for the date. (This point of view may be considered old school, and times have changed a bit. Today, some women have no problem splitting the bill or even covering the bill. She may offer to pay from time to time, and if so, you can decide if you'd like to accept it. Never expect it.)

- Even though women are independent, they still love flowers, or to be invited to nice restaurants. NO, I'm not trying to hear that you can't afford it. Showing the one you care about a good time is necessary. Just like you found a way to get those nice sneakers or that expensive phone, you can put a little cash to the side for your lady. Show her how important she is and that she is worth whatever it takes to make her happy.
- Always walk a woman to her car and make sure she gets home safely.
- Surprise her with random notes that say how thankful you are to be a part of her life. (Women love this. Major bonus points here).
- Show up well, always. Women loved clean, well-groomed men.

Ladies:

As a man, I will be the first to tell you that I am no expert on what women should or should not do when dating. I suggest that you find a woman you trust and ask questions about this.

But I will say this, use those tips that I gave to the gents above as your guide. If a man is not doing those things for you, then he is not worthy of your love or time. These are basic things that every man should know and do. If you are dating and not receiving respect, nice dates, love notes, and someone who takes the time to know you are safe, then that is not the man for you.

What I want you to know is you are valuable and precious. I want you to carry yourself that way. Hold your head up high, and never loosen your standards or expectations for how you want to be treated.

I give the same advice to young men as I give to you—present yourself as the woman who mirrors the man you want to attract. Show up well. Men love well-put-together women. They love women who speak well, are poised, work hard, and have goals and dreams. You have all of this going for you. Show it off.

Action Steps

Write out a list of characteristics and qualities you want the man or woman in your life to have. This is your checklist.

Once you review that checklist, you become that person on the checklist. We must be mindful that we cannot want this amazing person, without being that amazing person.

Keep Your Hands to Yourself

Any unwanted physical touch in a relationship is considered domestic abuse. Keep your hands to yourself. I understand arguments get heated, especially when we care about someone. But, if you care about them that much, the last thing you should be doing is causing them physical or emotional harm. Everyone deserves respect. You don't have a right to touch or hurt anyone just because you are upset.

If you find yourself in a physical situation with someone that is about to turn violent, walk away and take a few deep breaths.

Action Steps

Remember: Use your deep breathing techniques we talked about in the previous chapter. You must be slow to anger. Once you decide to raise your hand at someone during a domestic dispute, you leave no room for negotiation. You will go to jail.

Section Seven

Get Your Body Right

In my freshmen year, I was 6'2" and 148 pounds. I was skinny, I really wanted to try out for the basketball team. I had skills with friends, so I knew I was good enough to play for a team.

I tried out and made the team, but when it came to running drills and keep up with the other athletes, I couldn't do it. I was too unhealthy. I was slim, but my eating habits were terrible. Instead of eating foods that improved and nourished my body, I ate chips, candy, pop, juice, and every other fast snack I could grab. I didn't exercise at all, and it showed. That experience was eye-opening for me. I didn't completely change my lifestyle right away, but I slowly started making changes to eat better and work out more. As I got older, I became even more serious about my body, and today, I work out regularly. I am a personal trainer who help others to get fit and live healthier. I know for sure that health is important, and the healthier your body is, the stronger your mind is.

Health increases your energy and productivity so you can do more and as a result, earn more. This is why they say "Your health is your wealth." Successful people are known for being fanatical about their health. They make time to work out, eat well, drink water, and rest.

You don't have to wait until you are an adult to get serious about your health. You can start today.

We have talked about leadership in this book and the importance of setting an example. I am sure you have friends who are overweight or who may be skinny, but they are unhealthy. If you decide to get your health in order, think about what it would inspire others to do. Imagine…

- If you were the healthiest student in your school?
- If every sports team wanted, you to play for them because of your athletic build and muscles?
- If every student wanted to hang around you because they admired your dedication to the gym?

How would it feel to be a positive example for others and to be able to do the things you want to do physically?

I wish someone would have shared a plan to get healthy long before I found it out for myself. That's why I want to help you.

Let's get your body right!

Step 1: Identify your weight goal.

You need to know where you want to be to know what it takes to get there. Identifying your weight goal helps you to measure your progress and keep you on target. Decide how much you want to weigh.

Once you have identified your weight goal, weigh yourself. Track your weight by writing it down every day. It does not matter if you want to lose weight or gain weight, it is your personal preference. You should include the date you started, your current weight and the weight you want to be. Set a deadline to reach that weight goal.

Step 2: Proper dieting.

Diet is key. You cannot live how I was in my younger days, eating junk food and drinking pop, and expect to be healthy. A balanced diet will propel you to your ideal fitness goal. Fruits, vegetables, healthy proteins, whole grains, and water are considered a balanced diet.

You can have a "treat meal" here and there, but not a "treat" day. A treat meal is one meal you love, not a whole day of stuffing your face with ice cream, cake, cookies, and chips. Binges like this will set you back and erase all of your hard work and progress in a day. Enjoy foods you like occasionally, but try to stay committed to your goals.

If you want to learn more about dieting, consult with a nutritionist. Ask your nurse at school for a referral or ask a parent to make an appointment with a doctor or a certified dietician.

Step 3: Exercise.

You have to move your body to reach your weight goals. Exercising speeds up the process of either gaining weight or losing weight. Being active 2-3 times a week for at least 30 minutes is a great way to start a healthy lifestyle.

First, consult with a doctor to ensure you can perform various exercises. For beginners who want to lose weight, I would recommend walking on the treadmill for 21 days until your heart is conditioned for exercising. After you are comfortable with walking on the treadmill, start intervals of walking/jogging. The exercise will help burn calories, not just in the gym but throughout the day.

For beginners who want to gain weight, first, consult with a doctor to ensure that you are underweight and need to put on a few pounds. Many people want to gain weight or bulk up to achieve a certain look, which is not a great idea. You may be the right weight for your height, age, and gender. It is important to visit a doctor and get your accurate weight. Visit your doctor and let them know your plan. They will guide you in the right direction or inform you if this is the right thing for you.

You want to know your Body Mass Index or BMI. A doctor can help you find out your BMI and what your weight should be. It is very important that you know this information before you start gaining or losing weight.

Once you have the green light to gain weight, start gradually by increasing your calorie intake per day. It's okay to use a gym, but push-ups, sit-ups, and pull-ups are exercises that keep you lean. Plus, these can be done at home or in a park with exercise equipment. This is a good way to save money on gym memberships.

Step 4: Rest.

Muscle recovery is the name of the game. Resting is the stage where your muscles begin their recovery stage. However, during this resting period, it is important to stretch and drink plenty of water. This is not the time to have a treat meal or make mindless decisions about your choice of food. Remain focused on feeding your body healthy meals. Always ask yourself, "Is the food I am about to consume what champions eat?" If not, leave it alone.

Action Plan

1. Write out your plan for getting healthy.
2. Decide what your weight goal is.
3. Consult with a doctor to find out what your BMI is.
4. Consult with a doctor or nutritionist on what diets are best for you.
5. Find an exercise that you like and commit to it 2-3 times per week.
6. Rest on those alternate days.
7. Drink plenty of water.

Section Eight

Social Media Dos and Don'ts

Represent Yourself Well Online

Social media is one of those things that we cannot avoid or overlook. It's a part of our everyday lives, and a powerful tool for communication, connection, and knowledge. At some point during the day, be it for research, inspiration, catch up with friends, or search for jobs, we find ourselves on Instagram, Facebook, Snapchat, or LinkedIn (or maybe all of these) at some point during the day.

The fact that social media is so public and accessible is why we need to be mindful of how we use it. Yes, it's fun with friends, but you have to remember that whatever you post and share on social media is largely for the world to see. We have all seen stories of celebrities, athletes, and politicians who have tweeted or posted something that has come back to bite them and damage their careers. It didn't have to happen yesterday either. They could have made a bad decision years ago, and reap the repercussions of that statement or image today. A racist comment or a picture from a wild college party could cost someone their entire career. Take note: Think before you post anything. This applies even when your page or posts are private. You never know who is watching and screenshotting. Once you put something out online, it can be there forever—whether you delete it or not. You cannot move faster than a hater who is just waiting for a chance to damage your reputation.

Today, social media platforms are like resumes. Your pages and profiles can tell college recruiters and potential employers *a lot* about you and your life. They will use this information to determine if you are the right fit for their campus or office environment.

Let's look at some social media scenarios:

Scenario 1: John is an excellent student. His grades are great and he graduated with honors. He was valedictorian of his class. John had a list of great schools he wanted to apply to, he was set to head to college after graduation.

John was a great student, but he was popular too. He liked to hang out and party with friends on the weekends. He constantly posted unflattering pictures of himself and his friends, drinking and smoking weed. He would curse in some of the posts and he used a derogatory slur here and there too. But he thought it was harmless and funny. They were just having fun.

When it was time for John to apply for college, he did not realize that his social media pages could be a problem. He applied his dream schools, and we were certain he would get into all of them. He told a guidance counselor about his applications, and he suggested that he consider deleting some of those images from his social media right away. Scared that his future could be in jeopardy, John rushed home after school to clean up his accounts. But it was too late.

A week later, John received rejection letters from all the schools he applied to. With his grades and other achievements, there is no reason why he should have been denied. He was crushed.

John's father was the dean of admissions to one of the schools John applied, The two saw each other at an event, and John's dad mentioned that his son had applied to his school, but wasn't accepted. The dean knew immediately why. He shared with John's father that John's behavior outside of school "did not represent the type of student they would want on their prestigious campus." Social media it was.

Now John must find another school to attend. He missed an opportunity of a lifetime due to his public profile.

Scenario 2: Kelly graduated from college and is searching for a job in her field of counseling. She volunteers her time and resources to underperforming and impoverished communities. She also donates to non-profit organizations in the city she lives in. She shares her positive work on social media to inspire others to give back.

When Kelly applied for a job at a well-known nonprofit, they wanted to know more about her. The recruiter went to her social media feed and was impressed with what she saw. There was picture after picture of Kelly with the kids she mentored, feeding the less fortunate, passing out turkeys on Thanksgiving, and wrapping presents on Christmas to give to children at a local shelter. Impressed, the company called Kelly in for an interview and offered her a high-paying position.

In this instance, social media helped Kelly to get the job she desired.

Social media can hurt or help you. If you don't want people to misjudge you, keep that in mind when you post. If you want to keep your private life private, do not post. Social media is not intended to be your daily journal (I know, I know. There are a lot of people who use it that way.) But you cannot expect to put everything out there about your life, relationships, breakups, highs, and lows, and then wonder why people are "in your business." The world only knows what you tell it.

Take a note from successful businesses and celebrity entrepreneurs who have leveraged social media to build brands and ultimately, to make money. A brand is what people think about you and perceive you to be, and, in today's world, brands are largely determined by social media. You have one, whether you know it or not.

When people come across you online, what do you want them to think about you? What do you want them to know about you? If a school, employer, mentor, or someone you were hoping to impress found your Facebook page, would it be a good representation of you?

If the answer is "no", consider cleaning up your social media. Start posting more positive aspects of your life, such as your achievements, positive pictures with your family and friends, your graduation and prom. Leave posts about fights with friends, people who are getting on your nerves, and violent videos that have gone viral off your page.

Don't give anyone an opportunity to misjudge you based on a small sliver of your life that they see online. The truth is, you can't always control what people think, but you can make it difficult for them to form a negative opinion about you by controlling what they see and hear. If they are going to talk, be sure their only option is to say something good.

Action Steps

Go through all of your social media accounts and audit them. Ask yourself these questions:

1. What is my brand? How do I want to be known personally, academically, and professionally?
2. Does this post represent my brand well?
3. Whenever the answer is "no", delete the post.

Be sure to complete this exercise before you apply to any college, jobs, or major opportunities.

Be in the moment

Try to hang out with friends without being on social media, Snapchatting, going live, or scrolling down your news feed. Just enjoy the moment with your friends, family, or significant other. Taking pictures to remember the  experience is great and recording views are awesome as well. But many of us get carried away with being on the phone instead of just enjoying the moment.

The reason you have friends and family is to enjoy each other's company, have fun, and create memories. Try to minimize your social media usage when you are out. I am sure it will be hard, but it is worth it.

Spend less time posting pictures of your dinner plate, your location, and your outfit of the day, and more time enjoying your meal, laughing, and having a good time with the person you are with. (Unless you are a blogger or influencer, then posting is how you get paid. So, in that instance, you must do it. But I am certain even they take a break from their phone at least one hour a day.)

Be mentally, physically, and emotionally present when on dates and with friends and family. You never know when you will get that opportunity again. Life is not always promised.

Look around, smell the aromas, listen to the birds chirping and the wind blowing, tune into conversations, ask questions. Just be there with no distractions.

Action Steps

The next time you are out with people you care about, consider leaving your phone in the car. I know, it will feel weird at first, but trust me, you will enjoy your evening a lot more when you are not checking your social media and messages once every 2-3 minutes. The person or people you are with will enjoy the time with you too.

Section Nine

I Have My Driver's License, How Do I Keep It?

You got your driver's license. Congratulations! That is a major milestone in life and it's exciting to be more independent.

Being a young driver can be intimidating. You have heard all those stories about accidents, drunk drivers, cars being towed or taken away by the police. As a teenage driver, you have strict rules. In this section, we will discuss some ways to be sure that does not happen.

Driving While Distracted: Don't Do It!

Distracted driving is terrible (and illegal). I know you have seen people multi-tasking while driving and managed to not get caught or cause an accident, but that's no reason for you to mimic that bad and irresponsible behavior.

Texting and Cell Phones: First and foremost, texting and driving is a Huge No…. No! I know everyone does it, but that does not make it right. Driving and texting is illegal and dangerous. Having a conversation via text message is not more important than your life or anyone else's. In Illinois, if a police officer catches you texting and driving, or you cause an accident as a result. You will be issued a citation for the first offense, the second offense in that same year could suspend your license, then revoked.

In Illinois and other states, you can get a moving violation for simply holding a cell phone in your hand. You do not need to be texting or talking to break the law.

Things happen in a split second; one minute you are texting and the next you are involved in an accident. I am speaking from experience. Once I was stopped at a red light when I left school and started to text. I looked up and the light turned green, but the cars were still stopped. My focus was on the phone. The car in front of me had not started moving yet, and I ran into the back of a woman's car. It was a careless mistake that could have been avoided if I were paying attention.

Always remember: If it is that important, pull over. No one is more important than your life or the life of someone else.

Distracted Driving: There are a lot of reasons that cause us to take our eyes off the road, and none of them are good. Putting on makeup, entertaining friends while driving, looking at Snapchat, Facebook, Instagram, or watching YouTube or other social media platforms while driving are all wrong. Distracted driving can endanger many people's lives, including pedestrians, bicyclists, other motorists, and yourself.

Although most drivers who get pulled over for driving distracted are between the ages of 16-24, people of all ages are found guilty of this. Remember, that conversation or YouTube video is not more important than your life or anyone else's life.

Why the Earbuds?

Lose the earbuds or headphones while driving. Driving with earbuds is illegal in Illinois. If you have them in both ears and there is an emergency vehicle (police car, ambulance, or fire truck) behind you, there is a possibility that you will not hear them. Be aware of everything that is going on around you to keep yourself and others safe.

Earbuds are dangerous even while waiting for the bus, walking around campus, or traveling on public transportation. Always be aware of your surroundings . Keep your ears (and eyes) open and alert.

What Are You Listening to That Is So Important?

I am sure the cost of the phone or the headache of filing a police report is not worth it. I have responded to countless reports by students who were victims of robberies and theft because of earbuds. I'm not saying the earbuds or headphones were the cause, but when you are distracted it makes you more vulnerable to becoming a target or victim.

Working out or at home is a great place to utilize earbuds because you are in a safe environment. However, using them at other times, like when you are walking home at night alone, makes you a target. The thief can walk up behind you without ever being heard.

Drunk driving: I am sure this is not something you would ever do, but I will address this just so you are aware. Driving drunk is unsafe for you, your passengers, other motorists, and pedestrians.

One unwise decision to drink and drive could cost you thousands, or your life or someone else's.

Driving while intoxicated can result in arrest, expensive tickets and fines, losing your license, and your car. If you are pulled over and suspected of driving drunk, the officer may require you to take a breathalyzer test to determine your blood/alcohol level right there on the spot. This is humiliating and scary.

If you are required to go to court for a hearing, a judge may order that a device be installed in your car to measure your blood/alcohol level before you start your car. You will have to blow into a tube to start your car. The car will not start if your breath test is over the limit. You will need to blow into a tube. If you try to have someone else blow in this tube for you, it will cost you and that person jail time along with a hefty fine. In addition, there is a cost of $60-$90 a month to lease the device.

Driving drunk is costly. Think about this before you do it.

When traveling with passengers, be smart about who you let in your car. Before allowing someone in your car, ask if they have any illegal weapons or drugs with them. If you are letting someone borrow your car, ask to see their driver's license. Again, make sure you trust the person and they are responsible.

Car accidents are inevitable. Practically everyone with a driver's license has been involved in at least one accident in their lives. It happens. However, you can minimize your risk by not drinking and driving, absolutely no texting while driving, and obeying the traffic laws.

Speeding is not good, especially if you get caught. If you get pulled over by a police officer for speeding and your license gets taken away, it may cost you approximately $175 for the speeding ticket and the offense will be on your record. This would also raise your car insurance premium. More importantly, if you get your license suspended or revoked it can cost thousands of dollars to get your license back in good standing again. In short, monitor your spending and drive with due regard for safety.

Speaking from experience, I was caught speeding when I was 18 years old. Although my licenses were not suspended, I paid a hefty amount to keep them. I had to do volunteer work for a week, and I was on probation until 21 years old. Which means I could not receive any tickets during this time. (*Read your Rules of The Road handbook in your state.*)

Speeding is not worth it. Obey the law.

Action Steps

Remember these rules:

1. When you start driving, minimize the passengers in your vehicle unless they are your parents or responsible adult.
2. Always wear your seatbelt along with your passengers.
3. Although it is difficult to drive and monitor your passengers, periodically glance to see what they are doing. Ex. You could be driving, and your backseat passenger could be drinking alcohol in the back seat. This incident could cost you big bucks. Be responsible.

4. Keep your music at a minimum. In Chicago, this can get you a ticket and car towed.
5. Always keep your eyes on the road. If you drop something leave it on the floorboard or pull over.

Just Say No!

In high school and college, you will be tempted to experiment with a lot of new things—including drugs. Unfortunately, it's inevitable that someone will attempt to convince you

to try alcohol or illegal drugs. **DO NOT** let your curiosity get the best of you. Resist temptation and just say "**NO**." Drugs can not only take your license. They can take your health and your life.

I understand you want to fit in and do what the popular people are doing. I understand peer pressure and wanting to have more fun. I understand you may want to self-medicate pain from a sports injury. I also understand why you think using drugs would increase your energy so you can stay up longer to study and boost your grades. You may have watched your friends use drugs for these reasons and you think you should too. However, you need to understand that many of these scenarios lead to deaths, addiction, and abuse among teens and young adults.

According to a teen rehab center, "10% of "A" students smoke marijuana compared to 48% of "D" and "F" students." That tells me that most "A" students are making better decisions when it comes to using marijuana and leaving the drugs alone. According to one study, experts found that 12th graders who smoke marijuana are 65% more likely to be involved in an automobile crash. Leave drugs alone. They are not worth taking your grades or your life.

Prescription drugs are still illegal if they have not been prescribed to you. These are some of the popular drugs that students come across and should always stay away from unless they are prescribed by your doctor:

- Adderall
- Opioid painkillers
- Vicodin
- OxyContin
- Inhalants
- Ritalin

Ecstasy (MDMA) and LSD are also popular street and party drugs that should be avoided at all costs. These drugs are highly addictive and impair your judgment, which is particularly dangerous while driving or in social situations. Anything that affects your brain in a negative way impairs your learning and makes it difficult for you to make decisions is bad a thing. Stay away from it.

Young people make sure you know what you are getting into. Your life is not worth it.

Growing up, I knew a young man who grew up in the same neighborhood as I did. He was smart, athletic, and had a great family. But he started smoking marijuana and never was the same. We all slowly watched him mentally deteriorate. He stopped excelling in school and playing sports. He became delusional and lost his memory. He was never the same.

Marijuana and other drugs may seem harmless, but they are not. When you buy drugs, you have no idea what you are really purchasing and ingesting in your body. What you think is just weed or a pill could be a mixture of lethal substances with horrible consequences. Do not put your future on the line for something stupid. I know it's a different world and marijuana is legal in most states but be mindful that your age plays a significant role. Teenagers may have a different effect than an adult. Therefore, in most states, the legal age to purchase recreational marijuana is 21.

When you use drugs, you are one decision away from a situation that could cost you your health or your life. Electronic cigarettes and/or vaping is also harmful, it contains nicotine which is very harmful to brain development. *(know the risk before making these decisions.)*

Action Steps

I know there will be parties you want to attend. Go ahead, but be aware:

- Be mindful of what you drink. That punch you think is only Kool-Aid could be more than that.
- Be mindful that the air you breathe could be full of marijuana or any other dangerous drug. You may think just because you're not smoking it that it's not harmful. But second hand smoke is bad as smoking directly.
- Remember, you are one decision from helping your life or harming your life. If the doctor didn't prescribe it, then it's not for you.

Be Someone Your Parents Can Trust

I understand you are a young adult, but remember, your parents are responsible for you until you are 18 years old and considered a legal adult. Imagine how disappointed and embarrassed your parents would be if you got in trouble with the law or worse.

What if your parents read about something you did in the newspaper, see it on television, or hear it over the radio? What would that do to them?

Be responsible. It's the right thing to do, out of respect for your parents and yourself.

When your parents and other adults can trust you to be responsible, you will be rewarded with more freedom. Being responsible means: coming home within your curfew, hanging out with the right people, being a good driver by not speeding or running red lights and stop signs, doing your homework, cleaning your room and cleaning up after yourself when you made a mess on the kitchen table.

Being responsible is all about doing the right thing when no one is watching – not just when someone is around paying attention.

Do you want to know what worries your parents the most? It's not that you will always get good grades, be a good athlete, or be popular. It's that you are safe and growing into a responsible adult. Your parents want to know that they are raising you to make good decisions so you can take care of yourself, whether they are around or not. They breathe a lot easier when you show them you are responsible.

Let me be clear, I wasn't a saint growing up. I remember when my mother told me to stay away from a certain crowd and, of course, I did not. I thought I was slick by going behind her back and hanging out with them.

One night, I was set up by someone I knew. I never hung out with the person; we just knew each other. He told me to meet him somewhere but unbeknownst to me, he told the security guard I was coming to get a weapon. Fortunately, I was able to get out of that situation, but I could have easily gone to jail.

I wanted to fit in. I wanted to be in the "*IN*" crowd, but that one irresponsible decision could have landed me in prison. But I had a praying mother that always kept me covered. (Thanks, Mom.)

Always remember: Before you decide to do something wrong, think about the repercussions. Think about yourself. Think about your future. And think about the people who love you.

Action Steps

Here are some tips to keep you safe when hanging out:

- Next time you leave the house, let your parents or guardian know where you're going and who you're going with.
- Once you arrive give them a courtesy call that you arrived safely.
- Then, when your headed home let them know you're on your way. This may seem too much, but your parents will be happier and at ease knowing you're okay.
- If location changes, give them an update.

Know-a-days, knowing that our loved one is safe is very crucial.

Interacting with a Police Officer

You should always remember that every person in law enforcement is not out to get you. All officers are not perfect, but in these scenarios, the officer is the person of authority. You must be  respectful and responsible and do everything you are asked to do. Your goal is to get home safely.

If you are ever pulled over or approached by the police, stay calm. Let the officer do their job. If you haven't done anything wrong, there is no reason to panic.

Follow these tips too:

- Do not run when approached or questioned by the police. Despite what you have heard, the most unreasonable thing you can do is run from a police officer. If you have not done anything wrong, why run?
- Keep your voice at a respectable level.
- Always remain respectful , even if the police officer raises his voice and uses derogatory language.
- DO NOT try to win an argument on the street. Again, remain respectful and do what you are told.

- Always keep your hands visible. ***This will ensure you are no threat to the officer.***
- You should also try to write down or remember the officer's badge number, last name, location, and time of day.

If you are under 18 years old, address the officer with your parent. DO NOT do this alone. Advise the officer you want to speak to them with your parents.

I want you to be prepared, not scared when you have to interact with the police. Let's walk through a few scenarios so you know what to do if you find yourself in these situations:

Scenario #1

You are pulled over by the police.

What Should You Do:

1. Turn down the music and keep your hands on the steering wheel until the officer approaches and gives you directions.
2. Remain calm and courteous; your actions and attitude can negatively or positively impact the outcome.
3. If the officer asks for your driver's license, insurance card, and registration, let the officer know where and what you are reaching for.

4. It is okay to ask why you are being stopped. However, if the officer neglects to tell you, continue being courteous and follow directions. Meanwhile, make note of the badge number and the name of the officer. Report the traffic stop to their supervisor and the officer misconduct division. DO NOT handle this without your parent or guardian; having an adult with you during this process will make the situation run smoothly and effectively.
5. Never resist arrest. On the street is the wrong time to prove your innocence. Do what the officer tells you to do, and then follow-up accordingly.

Bonus Tips: Know who and what is always in your car when you are carpooling. Also, avoid playing music too loud. These can either cause you to get pulled over or escalate a situation once an officer stops you.

Scenario #2

You and a group of friends are hanging out in front of your house, and a police officer drives down the street. The officer notices you just hanging out, and he stops to speak to you and your friends.

What You Should Do:

1. First, Do Not Run! From an officer's point of view, only guilty people run.

2. The proper way to engage with the officer is to acknowledge them with a wave or speak to them. This will lower the officer's guard as they approach. The officer might say, "Hi, what are you guys up to? Do you live here?" Your reply would be," Yes officer, I live here."
3. Explain to them what you are doing, whether it be hanging out or waiting for friends.

Be mindful that the officer might be responding to a call or just patrolling. However, remember the officer is doing their job. What if that officer passed a group of people in front of a house, did not stop to question them and later you found out that a group of people was planning a burglary? I know some officers might have other motives, but most officers are public servants and are being proactive in the community by investigating.

Scenario #3

An officer responds to a fight at your high school. The only information the officer has received is… that there is a huge fight at the school. There will probably be a lot of police officers responding.

What Should You Do:

1. Do not assume the officer is aware of who is involved.

2. Again, DO NOT RUN! Stay calm and cooperate. The officer might be alarmed because of the environment. It is loud, with a lot of people screaming, arguing, videotaping, etc.
3. Be kind! Help the officers identify the people involved in the fight. Do not look at it like you are snitching, see it as doing a good service for your school, community, friends and yourself. You can do this anonymously. You will be identified as a hero. You can help your school be a safer place.

In this scenario, keep in mind that the officer may be a bit uncomfortable as well as vulnerable. Why? I am glad you asked.

The officer might be a new police officer with limited experience, and it can be intimidating working with youth. In this case, the officer is unfamiliar with school culture, but more importantly, they may not have been in this situation before or was involved in another case where the incident turned out badly. When that officer shows up at your school, help ease their temper by assisting them instead of verbally attacking them. Officers are just like you and me. They are citizens; that is where the word 'cop' comes from (*Citizen on Patrol*). I am not completely sure this is true, but I like saying this. (*LOL.*)

An encounter with the police in your lifetime is inevitable. Chances are the outcome will always be positive. You can increase the likelihood of avoiding conflict and negative outcomes with the police by keeping cool, being respectful, and working with your parents to handle anything the officer have done that violated your rights.

Action Steps

- Go to your school resource office and get to know that officer.
- Go to your local police department's CAPS office and get to know the officers in the community. Especially the officers who patrol around your school and home.
- Wave to police officers passing by. (This really does make officers feel appreciated because most of the time they are getting the finger, and I'm not talking about the thumbs up)
- Flag them down to have a friendly conversation. Ask them about their day. Add "How do they like being an officer?" and ask what safety tips they could recommend for the neighborhood.

Remember, conversations change situations. If an officer has a friendly relationship with you, chances are he would approach you, your neighborhood, and your community differently.

You Need Insurance

If you are driving a car, it needs to be insured. In fact, any vehicles on wheels (cars, trucks, motorcycles, and other road vehicles) should be insured.

Your parents may cover your insurance policy, or you may have to pay for your own. Car insurance, also known as vehicle, motor, or auto insurance) provides financial protection against physical damage or bodily injury resulting from traffic collisions and against liability that could also arise from incidents in a vehicle. Vehicle insurance may additionally offer financial protection against the theft of the vehicle, and against damage to the vehicle sustained from events other than traffic collisions, such as keying, weather or natural disasters, and damage sustained by colliding with stationary objects.

There are typically two types of car insurance:

Liability Insurance: Liability insurance (also called third-party insurance) is a part of the general insurance system of risk financing to protect the purchaser (the "insured") from the risks of liabilities imposed by lawsuits and similar claims. It protects the insured in the event he or she is sued for claims that come within the coverage of the insurance policy. Originally, individual companies that faced a common risk formed a group and created a self-help fund out of which to pay compensation should any member incur loss (in other words, a mutual insurance arrangement). The modern system relies on dedicated carriers, usually for-profit, to offer protection against specified risk in consideration of a premium. (Wikipedia, 2019)

Full Coverage Insurance

Full coverage provides more protection. This coverage ensures that your car will get fixed or replaced after being involved in an accident.

Full coverage may cost more than liability insurance, but the peace of mind is well worth it.

For example, John was on his way home from work when he was hit by another motorist (a.k.a. another driver). John had full coverage but the motorist who struck John did not. Thankfully, John had full coverage. He was able to get his vehicle fixed, and although he had to pay a deductible it was much less than buying a new car.

Now, if John would have had liability insurance only, he would be stuck paying for his damaged vehicle if the other motorist was uninsured.

The cost for full coverage depends on the year and make of the vehicle. The newer the car, the more insurance you want to carry on it. As your car gets older, full coverage can cost more than what the car is worth. In that case, you may decide to only cover the car with liability insurance.

Having car insurance is not only state law in every state, but it is also necessary to cover expenses in case of an accident. Liability covers another party's vehicle when you are in an accident, whether it's property damage or physical damage. NOT having insurance could cost you a major fine and possibly a lawsuit filed against you by the other party. (Wikipedia , 2019)

Action Steps

- Shop around for insurances. Some insurances charge a high premium because of your age. Don't go with the first company you see, do your research.
- Ask for student discounts or keep insurance in your parent's name to cut costs.
- Look for incentives for being a responsible driver. Some insurance companies cut you a check every year for being a safe driver. How cool is that? Get paid for doing the right thing.
- Having insurance is mandatory in all states, getting caught without it can cost you a few hundred the first time, second time thousands.

Section Ten

Making Your Own Money

Work Part-Time While in School

If you are old enough to read, you are old enough to work. Your high school and college years are expensive, and if you have dreams of your own car, senior pictures, a LIT prom, senior trips, and graduation parties, that money must come from somewhere. If you need money, you must work.

No, not necessarily hard, but smart.

I was fortunate to have an older cousin who helped me secure a part-time job at Subway while in 8th grade. I would work as many hours as the manager would let me after school and on the weekends. I could not receive an actual paycheck due to my age, so I was paid in cash. At the time, it didn't feel like I was giving up time to hang out with my friends and mess around, even though I was making that sacrifice. What I cared about was making my own money, and buying the things that I wanted, without having to ask my parents.

Having a job helped me learn how to manage my time and establish a great work ethic (which I still have now). I learned how to become independent and responsible at an early age, and I took pride in that. I was able to buy clothes, jewelry, and shoes. I even paid for my own graduation, something not too many eighth graders could say they did.

By my freshman year, I had saved enough money to purchase my first car. I could not drive yet because I was not old enough to have a license, but my brother and I took turns driving to school. By the time I was senior in high school, I had worked at least five different jobs. Let me tell you some of the biggest lessons I learned in that time:

Spend and save your money wisely. I get into this more in the next sections of this book, but I cannot stress the importance of learning good money management early enough. I made a lot of money as a kid, but I didn't know what to do with it. Instead of saving, my money went towards buying things of no value such as cars which I could not drive, jewelry, clothes, shoes, rims, television for my car and loudspeakers for my car stereo. It was fun while it lasted but looking back, I should have made better choices. If a book like this existed when I was younger, it would have provided me with a better understanding and direction.

I wish someone told me to save more so I could invest later. I wish someone had told me about the 70% rule—live off of 70% of your income, save 10%, invest 10%, and give 10%.

Think about it like this: If you make $250, you should give $25, save $25 and invest $25.00.

I know you are thinking, "I'll get around to saving and investing when I get older." But any adult who has suffered the financial consequences of poor money management will tell you this is the wrong way to think.

The best time to start following this basic rule is now when you don't have much. If you can master this now, it will be easier for you to apply the same rule as your income continues to grow.

Savings and investing are for you and your future. You need money put away for emergencies and unexpected expenses and opportunities that come your way.

Investing in finding ways to grow your money so you can generate wealth (without working for it) that will benefit you for years to come. Having a job and living at home is the perfect set-up for investing. As a teenager, you won't have many bills, other than a cellphone (if that). So, you can afford to invest more money in assets, like real estate and stocks, and allow them to grow in value.

Giving is for your future too. Giving back a part of what you earn is a principle that wealthy people live by. They understand that we all have a responsibility to help others and that whatever you give away will come back to you tenfold. Always remember it is better to give than to receive.

I am sure if you made $1 million dollars and you had to give $100,000 to a charity, you would have a problem with that. But practice with the smaller amounts of your income now. When it's time to write those big checks, you won't think twice about it. In fact, it will be a habit and you will be happy to do it.

Find a job you enjoy. You don't have to hate your job. Find a job that you don't mind going to. You should like the work and the people. Benefits like store discounts and tuition reimbursement are great too. Money is important, but your happiness is paramount.

Show up professionally. It doesn't matter how much you are getting paid to do a job, always be professional. That means showing up on time, well-dressed and well-groomed, and with a positive attitude and ready to work. Be trustworthy and responsible.

Action Steps

Every day, your job is to find a job until you get the one you want. Start calling, stopping by and emailing the places you want to work. Don't wait for them to contact you, to them you are only a number. Be persistent and know what you want.

Attend job fairs, seminars, talk with people about the job you want. Be willing to volunteer.

Always have a hard copy of your resume and a zip/flash drive with your resume on it. That way anyone can look at it or you can always send it to them on demand.

Go online and start searching for jobs that interest you. Indeed.com, ziprecruiter.com, and LinkedIn.com are great places to start. Craigslist is also a resource for local jobs.

What Does Your Email Say About You?

You need an email address, and if you are emailing anyone in a professional setting, you want to use an email address that indicates you are professional too. sexychocolate69@gmail.com is fine for your friends and personal use, but don't use anything creative or degrading for the email you use to conduct any kind of business. Here are some better alternatives:

- Use first name last name @ gmail.com
- Use last name first name @ gmail.com
- Use first initial last name @ gmail.com

Keep in mind your email will be seen by employers, teachers, advisors, coaches, and other professionals. You don't want anyone to get the wrong impression about you.

Action Steps

If you haven't already, create a professional email.

When creating professional emails, try your best to stay away from numbers. Names and initials are a safer way to go.

It's okay to have a personal and professional email create both.

Preparing for your job interview

The ability to communicate your skills, education, and abilities with a potential employer is critical. There is one sure thing about interviews: The more you have, the better you become at them. It can be unnerving to be in the spotlight and to have everything you say and do be judged, but this is your chance to really shine. It is the last hurdle. If you land this job, there will be no more applications, no more resumes, and no more following up on every lead. Go in there and knock out the other 10 hopeful candidates that are just as bright and eager as you are. No pressure here!

First and foremost - be yourself. Let your integrity and good character come through with a genuine smile and a real willingness to make a difference.

Sincerity, or the lack of, is easy to sense. If you know the kind of work you want to pursue, make sure the jobs you apply to are aligned. Do not accept a job that is someone else's dream or just to get money. You probably won't be successful at it.

Before the job interview, write down some potential questions to ask the person interviewing you. You may want to ask:

- What will a typical day look like for me?
- What will your work schedule be? Ask for a copy of the job description.
- What are the benefits?

Also:

Arrive early. If you are 30 minutes early- you are on time. Never arrive at a job interview late. This is a rule to always follow. It shows consideration for someone else's time and your eagerness to work. If your interview is at 10:00 am, you should arrive at 9:30 am. *(I was taught: If you arrive at 10:00 am, then your considered late.)*

- Always smile and be polite.
- Stay off the phone *(turn it off or put it on silent.)*

Start with a handshake and eye contact. Always greet others with a firm handshake and look a person in the eyes when you talk to them. Eye contact shows not only your confidence, but it is a sign of respect.

Send a thank you note. Within 24 hours of your interview, always send a follow-up email thanking the person for taking the time to meet with you. This does not guarantee you will get the job, but it does make a great impression.

Action Steps

Before you go on your first interview, ask an adult to role-play with you so you can practice. Have the person ask you some sample interview questions so you can rehearse your responses. Some traditional questions an interviewer may ask are:

- How did you learn about this position?
- Why do you think you would be a good fit for this role?
- Have you ever dealt with an upset customer or a difficult co-worker? How did you handle the situation?
- What do you consider your strengths and weaknesses?
- Why did you leave your last job?

A potential employer may or may not ask you these exact questions on every interview, but you want to be prepared.

Dress Like You Want the Job

When dressing for an interview, always put your best foot forward.

Gents: Be clean-shaven, dress pants (pulled-up), dress shirt, tie, sport coat and dress shoes (no gym shoes).

Ladies: Make sure your appearance is neat and you are well-groomed. Wear a dark or neutral-colored blazer and slacks or knee-length skirt, low heels or flats, simple jewelry (such as a watch and small earrings). Keep your make-up minimal (the more natural the better). Strong perfumes and scents should also be kept to a minimum.

I know you don't want to hear this, but long nails, super long eyelashes, and brightly colored hair may not be considered professional in all work environments. Get the job first, and if you find it's a more creative environment, then you can express yourself as much as you'd like.

First impressions are most often the last impressions. What impressions are you leaving on people? Always make sure it is a good one because you never know when you may see that person again.

Action Steps

If you need help with your interview attire just ask your parents, your teacher, or a family member. Or go to a clothing store and ask a salesperson to help you pick out some items. *Make sure you tell them it's for a job interview.*

Your local Goodwill is also a place to shop for inexpensive items. Professional men and women clean out their closets all the time and donate work-appropriate clothing that is in great condition. Stop by and see what you see. You may be surprised at what you find.

Great Companies to Work For

There are several great companies to work for.

Starbucks is one of them. This company has been in business for years and is constantly expanding, which is a great thing. Starbucks offers excellent employee benefits such as matching your contributions to your 401K and they also offer employee stock programs. Beyond that, Starbucks employees also enjoy:

- Medical, dental and vision coverage
- Tuition reimbursement

- Paid vacation
- Store discounts

Note: *No, Starbucks is not paying for this ad. (I wish they were).*

Hotels: Become a front desk representative. With this position, you will have the opportunity to communicate with many guests and strengthen your communication skills. You also get perks for staying at the hotel, eating at the restaurants and other hotels they are affiliated with. You can also have some "ME-TIME" at the spas where they offer discounted rates for the employees.

Valet: I am certain we all love driving a nice car, but as a valet, you can get paid for it. Most 5-star restaurants have valet parking for their customers. Think about that car you always wanted to drive, now you get to drive it and get paid while doing it. You never know what car will pull up next. On top of your hourly rate, you have an opportunity to collect tips from customers.

Most park districts, car washes, and restaurants hire high school and college students.

Action Steps

- Identify where you want to work and why.
- Write out the pros and cons of each job you are considering.

Start Your Own Business

You are never too young to start your own business.

With some creativity, discipline, and willingness to sell yourself, you can easily start a business around something you love and be your own boss. You only need a vision, a plan, and to execute it.

If you want to start your own business, but have no ideas on what you could try, **YouTube** is a great place to explore business ideas and learn some new skills that you can leverage to create income for yourself.

Start Small but Dream Big

A business doesn't have to be elaborate or complicated. Your goal is to create revenue and have a vision that everyone can be a part of. If you find that you enjoy entrepreneurship, this may be your first of many businesses. Start small but dream big. There is always room to grow. Every major company you see today started somewhere. It takes patience, passion, and persistence.

Start a small business by doing things you love and using what you have right now. Most businesses solve a problem in the economy. What problem could you solve? Ex. Uber and Lift saw a need to step away from that bright yellow or green Taxicab. These two companies have a transportation service that will pick you up and drop you off at your destination without having to stand in the street flagging taxicabs.

Start a Bike Rental Business

For example, if you have a bicycle, try making money by renting it to friends or people that you know and can trust. Charge for the service based on a specified time limit, like $5 an hour.

Start a Video Game System Rental Business

If you own a PlayStation, Xbox, Wii, or any other gaming system, you can rent the system out to other people who would like to use it. Keep in mind – this should be someone you know and trust. You do not want someone to damage or steal your system.

For either of these rental businesses, you need a simple contract explaining the guidelines for the user.

A basic contract should include:

- The customer's contact information. Verify the information they provide by comparing it to their picture identification (like a school I.D.) This will ensure you can track this person down if they fail to comply with your contract.

- Clear guidelines. The guidelines should be short, simple and clear. They should state what item you are allowing this person to borrow (bike, video game or system). State that you want the item returned exactly how you gave it to them.

If the user returns the item damaged or does not return the item at all, they will have to replace the item at full value. Again, I highly recommend you only conduct business with someone you trust and who will respect your item.

When the customer signs the contract, make sure their parents are aware of the business transaction. Make sure the parent signs next to their child. The parent's signature is proof that they are aware of the guidelines. Make sure all parties have a copy.

Start a Cleaning Business

You can start a cleaning business by purchasing cleaning supplies from a dollar or supply store. There is no degree or special training to learn how to clean. There are many people who are unable, busy or unwilling to clean their house, apartment, garage or business.

Start a Landscaping Business

You can make a fortune with a lawnmower and rake. If you can get at least five people on your block or in your neighborhood that can be a great start. Charge $50 a month to rake the leaves during the fall, shovel snow in the winter and cut grass in the summer.

Do the math:

- Monthly profit $200.00
- Yearly profit: $2,400

Not bad, right?

Start a Car Wash Business

You can start this business easily by yourself or with a friend. All you need are a few supplies:

- Soap
- Drying towels
- Tire shine
- Handheld vacuum
- Air freshener

These things can be found at a local auto store or possibly dollar stores.

Do the math:

- Per car: $10
- Weekly profit: $ 50.00 (5 cars per week)
- Monthly profit: $200.00

- Yearly profit: $2,400.00

The best time to take advantage of this opportunity is while you are young. People love paying young people to do something positive to make money. You have everything to gain and nothing to lose. Yes, it will require transportation, but you can walk or ride your bike.

If you do not own a bike, you can buy one for a couple of hundred dollars, or less. If you do not have that amount of money saved, ask a family member or friend for a loan with an agreement to repay the loan in a timely fashion. Draw up a contract with a monthly payment and what date the loan will be paid in full.

To get your business started, find customers in your neighborhood (i.e. churches, schools, neighbors, businesses, and park districts).

Get Paid to Take Surveys

Survey Junkie is a research company that pays up to $75 a survey. Wait…what? $75 for a survey? YES, that is correct.

All you need is to register and start completing surveys to earn $75. The great thing about Survey Junkie is you can complete surveys on your time. You do not need to get out of bed, stay out late at work, or deal with traffic. In fact, you do not even need to fill out an application or deal with a supervisor.

Another online survey company to consider is InboxDollars.Com.

Get Paid to Deliver Groceries

InstaCart is an option if you have your own car. You can get paid between $10-$20 an hour to shop for others and deliver their groceries. The average hourly rate is $10 per hour, but tips could boost the hourly rate to $20 an hour.

Get Paid to Save

Long Game Savings encourages people to build their savings. You can play games and win cash prizes to help with saving money.

Buy and Sell Domain Names

What about buying and selling domain names? Domains are like real estate—a person cannot create a "home" online (also known as a website) without a domain name.

The key here is to watch what's trending (like hashtags) and buy the domain from a site like Go Daddy, where you can purchase a domain for as low as $10. You would hold the domain, and if someone wants to buy it from you, they will have to put in a bid for you to accept. You could easily charge thousands for a domain.

Think about it—what if you had purchased a domain name like Facebook, Google, or Apple? If you purchased this domain name years before they were introduced to the world, those founders would have paid you millions to buy the domain name from you.

Action Steps

- Think about a business you can start with a few friends.
- Identify what supplies you need to make it work.
- Think about how much you would charge.
- Think about the need for the business, is it in high demand or can people live without it?

Think About a Real Estate Business

The real estate field offers plenty of lucrative business opportunities for entrepreneurs.

Here are a few to consider:

- Realtor
- General contractor
- Home Inspector
- Appraiser
- Property Management
- Maintenance Service/Handyman

Section Eleven

Get Your Money Right

I got my first credit card at eighteen years old. It was from a jewelry store, and when the salesperson told me I'd been approved, my heart was beating so fast, you'd thought I'd just won a million dollars. I had been in the store for thirty minutes, looking through the glass at all kinds of watches, chains and rings I could not afford. But that card changed everything. Within an hour, I had maxed out the entire $1200 limit on the card. It took ten years for me to pay off that balance.

I was only making the standard monthly payments, which were $25.00. The interest rate on the card was more than 20 percent, which is ridiculous, and that meant that most of my payment was going towards interest and not the $1200 balance. Over the course of ten years, I paid more than double what I had originally charged due to the high-interest rate. That was like throwing money out of a window, particularly since I could not find that watch today if you paid me. It's come and gone, just like a lot of hard-earned money that I've lost as a result of not knowing anything about managing money, budgeting, credit, and other important financial information. I knew nothing about the danger of debt, and why it was stupid to buy expensive liabilities such as fancy wheels for my fancy car, jewelry, and clothes. I spent and spent when I should have been saving and saving (and investing in assets, like real estate, to grow my money.)

This section is a crash course about money, based on everything I wish I'd known about finances when I was in my teens and early twenties. I know, from personal experience, that a lack of financial knowledge can cost you millions of dollars over the course of twenty years. The decisions you make today can be the difference between you living the life of your dreams in your thirties or struggling to survive with a bunch of debt and jacked up credit. You have a clean slate when it comes to your finances. I don't want you to mess that up.

Some of this information may not be applicable to you now, but I want you to at least be familiar with these concepts so you can make the best possible decisions when it comes to your finances. Apply what you can now and come back to this book when you have questions about big purchases, business opportunities, or investing. Everything I share here is just the tip of the iceberg, so go online, ask your mentors, and read books to learn more about these topics.

Your bank account will thank you later.

You Need A Budget

One of the first steps to organizing your finances is to set up a budget. You need to know exactly how much you make from your paycheck and how much of that money you spend. Your budget should include everything you pay for, including housing, utilities, clothes, food, and of course a little fun.

If you are planning on going to college, you should include your school expenses and create a college budget. If you are employed, prepare a monthly budget from your earnings at your job. Know how much income you have coming in every month.

Estimate expenses for every month based on your current bills and upcoming expenses. If you want to move into a new apartment, how much do you need to put towards a deposit? If your car needs tires, how much are they? If you want to take a trip with friends this summer, how much do you need for your flight and hotel? These expenses are a part of your budget. You don't want to leave anything out. If you don't plan for expenses, you'll spend money that you don't technically have, and find yourself in trouble. (*This is the main reason people have credit card debt.*)

In addition to helping you prioritize your expenses; a budget will help you save for the future and stay out of debt. The more savings you have, the more you can invest or do what makes you happy.

Ready to create your budget? Let's go!

1. The first step to creating a budget is tracking your spending. For one month, write down everything you spend, even small purchases like a soda or pack of gum. At the end of the month, categorize your expenses, and add up how much you spent for each. You should have a category for housing (if you pay rent), food, entertainment/fun, school, car, and miscellaneous. Miscellaneous could be self-maintenance, like haircuts, hair styling, or manicures/pedicures. Anything you can go without for a few months could be categorized as Miscellaneous.

2. Next, identify your income. Include paychecks, tips, and even gifts or birthday money. It is important to have a clear picture of what you are working with so you can create a realistic plan.

3. Finally, plan for your expenses. Expenses are either fixed or variable. Fixed expenses are always the same, such as car or insurance payments. Variable expenses, such as gas, entertainment or extracurricular activities are a little harder to plan for because the amount changes. That is why

tracking your expenses is so important. It will give you an accurate estimate of what you spend over time.

Also, plan for unexpected expenses such as an accident, car repair and hospital stay. You should have savings to cover these expenses as they come up. Stay tuned; we will get to that in the next section.

After walking through all the steps above, you should know two numbers, your income, and your expenses. Once you know your expenses, every month your goal is to stay within your budget.

Action Steps

Budgeting takes time and commitment. So, set aside a few hours this week to work on your budget. Be excited! This may seem like a tedious task but getting a handle on your money is so important. You are learning how to control your money and plant the seeds for living financially free in the years ahead. It all starts now.

Cash flow is keeping track of what money comes in and what money goes out. We spend money all day, from buying Hot Cheetos to catching an Uber ride home, cash is flowing from our hands for small and big things. It's very easy to lose sight of how much you're spending until you swipe that debit card and it declined. Therefore tracking your spending is so important. At all times you need to know how much cash you have on hand or in the bank. (i.e. savings, checking acct, bonds, credit cards)

Your cash flow is either positive or negative. If you bring home $1,000 a month in income, but your expenses are $300, that means you have a positive cash flow of $700 after all your expenses are paid. Great job!

Negative cash flow is not so good. If a person has a net income of $1,000 a month but has expenses that are $1,200 a month, they have a $200 negative cash flow, which means they are spending some of next month's earnings. This happens when you overspend, max out credit cards and take out loans you don't need *(which increases your monthly bills because of interest.)*

The way you can sustain a positive cash flow is first, you need income. *(Check out Section Ten, Making Your Own Money* to get started).

Once you are employed, start writing down your expenses.

- Add up all your bills including groceries and gas.
- If you are lending anyone money, this is an expense.
- Add up the amount you make every month (Net income).
- Subtract your expenses from your income. That will be your monthly cash flow number.

Example: If you have a Starbucks craving, love eating at Chipotle, or a cell phone bill, keep track of these expenses and how much you are spending. Don't hide it from yourself and not write it down. You want to know everything that is coming out of your account and what you are spending your money on.

If you get into a habit of tracking your cash flow at a young age, when you become a millionaire it will be easier to keep track of all your millions! Good luck!

Action Steps

When you get paid, give yourself an allowance. Think about how much you need for the next 2 weeks (which is payday). Once you identified the amount you need, take it from your banking account and keep it with you. We as consumers think twice about spending cash, but we love swiping the card. A set amount of cash in your wallet will help you control your spending.

Stop Spending So Much

If you are consistently spending more than you earn and you have negative cash flow, you have two options—earn more money or spend less. You must decide. But using credit cards, over-drafting your checking account, dipping into your savings, or borrowing money from family and friends are not answers to your problems. These are all bad habits that will come back to bite you. Figure out where your spending needs adjusting and commit to fixing it.

Sometimes you will need to spend less money. Take your own lunch to school or work. No, I am not talking about the lunch box you used in 3rd grade with Spiderman or Dora on the front. Get a grown-up, plain insulated lunch bag and pack your own lunch. This could save you or your parents thousands of dollars a year if you are still at home.

Cutting back on small things like lunch, snacks, and Starbucks can make a big difference overtime. If your parents don't have to give you lunch money every day, they may be able to afford a bigger graduation gift for you. If you save lunch money while at college or once you enter the work world, you can put what you save towards something you really want, like a car or a trip. A few dollars here and there add up over time.

Spending money on things that add little or no value is senseless. Save your money to purchase assets and not liabilities.

- Assets are things that make you money (i.e. real estate, stocks, and bonds).
- Liabilities are things that cost you money (i.e. cars, clothes, jewelry).

If you are scratching your head, no worries. By the end of this book, you will know the difference between the two, and you will be on your way to building great wealth.

Action Steps

1. Figure out where you can cut back.

2. Make your lunch at home instead of eating out.
3. Make your own coffee and tea instead of buying from a Starbucks or coffee bar at school or work.
4. If you would like to take it slow, start with cutting back on food and drinks a few times a week. Bring your own lunch for three days, and eat out on the other two days. Every little bit helps.

Save A Little

A penny saved is a penny earned. When I was thirteen, I got my first job at Subway. Earning $160.00 every two weeks as a young adult was great. Unfortunately, I spent it all on clothes and jewelry.

Do not make the same mistake.

If you have a job and income coming in, save some of your earnings. A good rule of thumb is to spend only 70% of your earnings and use 10 % for savings, 10% for investing and 10% for charity. If you continue this strategy with every dollar you make, you will be ahead of everyone around you. However, just because you may have more than the people around you doesn't mean they are beneath you, show them how you got there.

Remember, as you move forward in life, you must reach back and take others with you. Life is not about your income; it is about your impact.

If you start saving in high school, you will have more money to contribute to your college education. The more money you have, the more options are available to you in terms of colleges. You want to be able to attend the college that supports your interests, not just the college you can afford.

Action Steps

If it's hard for you to save, try this:

- When you purchase something in cash, save the change that is returned to you.
- When you are at the store, ask for a roll of quarters every time you get paid. That's a savings of $20 a month and $240 a year. Make sure you deposit the coins in a high-interest account, so you reap the benefits of compound interest. *(On-line saving accounts has the best interest rates)*

Have an Emergency Fund

One of the worst feelings in the world is being faced with an emergency and not having the funds to fix the problem or get yourself out of a crisis.

An emergency is an unplanned event such as:

- Repairing your car.
- Losing your job and still having bills to pay.
- Late paying rent, mortgage, or a car payment.
- A death in the family and need to help with paying the funeral expenses.

These are common situations that can cause financial distress for you if you are not prepared. You may have read this list and thought, "Oh, I would just ask my parents for the money! I'm good." If that is your response, then you need to pay attention to the pages that follow. It's great if you have parents, grandparents, or an older sibling who are willing and able to help you out of a bind. But your family is not a bank or an emergency fund. You are old enough to be independent, and that means you should be prepared to handle your own living expenses, at least as much of them as you can. I want you to begin to transition from being dependent to independent. It's time.

Maintaining an emergency savings account is a sign of independence and financial responsibility.

You should have three months of your monthly living expenses saved for an emergency fund.

For example, if you net (this is the amount of your paycheck that is left after you pay taxes to the government) $1,000.00 every month, you should have $3,000.00 in your emergency savings. This seems like a lot when you are starting from nothing, but believe me, if you focus more on the end of the journey versus the beginning, you will be there before you know it. There is something very satisfying about watching your money grow.

Building your savings means you can breathe when unexpected events come up. You will have the money stashed away and you can handle surprises without missing payments on your regular bills.

Be clear on what is considered an emergency and what is not. Don't be like me. I categorized everything as an emergency – from going out partying to buying a new pair of shoes. These are not legit emergencies.

Your emergency fund is for serious life events, not for fun. You should create a separate savings account for special items that you want to reward yourself with *(luxuries account.)* Decide what that item will cost, set a deadline for when you'd like to purchase it and divide the cost by the number of months you have to save. A little bit at a time!

Again: Save three times your monthly net income for your emergency fund.

Action Steps

Before you save for anything else, your emergency fund comes first. Add how much you make per month, times three and that's your emergency fund number.

Are you Ready to Have Your Own Car?

Oh, you want to be fancy, **HUH**??? So, you think you are ready to own your own car. Okay, let's talk about it.

The independence that a car offers is exciting. No more begging people for rides. No more waiting for someone to pick you up from school, work, or practice. No more expensive Ubers and taxis. Nobody all in your business… (Listen, if you are living under your parents' roof, they will be in your business, car or no car). Those are all benefits of having your own transportation. But a car does come with responsibilities—and expenses.

Before you go out and get that SRT Dodge Durango, Challenger, or Cherokee, look at your budget.

Ask yourself these questions:

- Does it make sense financially?

- How often will I drive, and how far am I driving?
- What will this car be used for?
- Can I afford the down payment, car insurance, gas, maintenance, and monthly car note?
- How will this purchase move me closer to my goals?
- Who is really winning in this situation, the car dealership or me?
- Also, look at what you will be paying after the term of the loan *(I am sure this will change your mind.)*

Well, I will answer that last one for you: the dealership and loan company are the ones winning.

The car loan will last for 7-8 years and accumulate about $10,000.00-$15,000.00 in interest. That means a $15,000.00 car could cost you $25,000.00-$30,000.00 in the long run. Keep in mind that your interest rates will be higher because you have no credit history.

Yes, you will be the popular "stud" or girl in school, but it will cost you. One alternative to purchasing a new car and saves your money would be buying a used car in good condition with cash, which should be your focus. You will have the benefit of no car note and a reliable car that should last you at least a few years if you maintain it well.

The instant gratification of a new car is not worth the cost. Those thousands of dollars that you would spend on a new car would be better off in your bank account. Before you jump into a big purchase like a car, think about your financial needs and goals.

Accumulate a nest egg (i.e. emergency fund, vacation fund and/or investment fund. Then, once you have established a solid savings fund, find an investment vehicle (real estate, stocks, bonds, etc.). Once you have these boxes checked, you can think about that brand-new car and enjoy it knowing that your financial future is headed in the right direction.

You Don't Have to Impress

We are all guilty of buying things to impress others, many of whom we don't even know. You don't need to keep up with others or buy fancy and expensive things to prove anything to anyone. This is the time in your life to be smart about your decisions and your money. I want you to apply the principles that you're learning in this book to set yourself up for the type of future that will allow you to live comfortably, and have some of the nice things you want, without having to go into debt or ruin your credit for them.

You do not need a closet full of designer jeans, the latest shoes, or the fanciest watch to get attention.

Stay away from the branding and logos that let the lookers know how often you wear your clothes. Several retail stores, such as T.J. Max or Marshalls, sell name-brand clothes at more affordable pricing. You can only wear one pair of pants at a time, and there are five school days a week. Purchase 5 pairs of pants and 14 shirts to rotate through the school year.

Look on the bright side: You are continually growing you will not be able to wear these clothes for long, which means you will need new clothes often.

Do you know what is an even better idea? Create your own clothing line and collect the profits.

I am not saying you should not look your best. I am saying there are other ways to look great without spending a ton of money. You can still stay fresh and well-groomed, with clean shoes, and still, look better than anyone in the room.

Your sense of style is what people will remember, not the brands you wear. People will remember your smile, your personality, and how well you treat them.

Action Steps

Your end goal is to save more and not impress more. Go to a department store such as Marshalls, TJ Maxx, or Ross. Purchase 5 pairs of jeans and 10 shirts. Try to find items with less noticeable logos. You will also need a pair of neutral-colored shoes (black, white, gray or tan) so they'll go with all of your new clothes.

Now that you have a nice, basic wardrobe, you can rotate your clothes throughout the week.

Checking and Savings Accounts

Once you start making money, you need somewhere to keep it. There are two types of banking accounts that every person should have, checking and savings.

Whether you are getting an allowance, student refund checks, getting a paycheck, or doing business, you will need two accounts. In any of these scenarios, you will typically have the option of receiving your funds through a direct deposit (an electronic deposit) or a paper check. In either instance, you will need a checking account to get access to your money as quickly as possible with a debit card or by going to the bank and withdrawing funds.

Having a checking account makes life very convenient. You can track your day-to-day spending, deposit and withdraw funds, send money and much more.

The only drawback to a checking account is the fact that your money does not accumulate interest as it sits in the bank. Interest is a percentage of your balance that the bank pays you as a reward for letting your money sit. The bigger your balance, the more interest you accrue. While you don't have this opportunity with checking accounts, you do with savings accounts.

For the money that you do not want to touch on a regular basis, you should put it in a savings account. Savings accounts do not have debit cards, so it's harder to get access to your money. This is a good thing! The key to savings is to set it and forget it. Make all deposits and limited withdrawals. Let your money grow and grow.

You should shop around for savings accounts to see what the best interest rate is.

In my opinion, online accounts are more profitable. The interest rates are higher.

Keep in mind that if you need to access funds from an online account, it may take a few days for the funds to be available. This is a long time, especially if you need it now.

When looking for a bank always consider:

- How close is the bank to your home/job?
- How many locations does the bank have?

- Can you bank from anywhere (i.e. home, school or your bed)?
- Can you access your bank balances?
- Can you deposit checks?
- Are you able to report fraudulent activity? How does the bank handle these scenarios?
- Can you connect to payment apps?

Do not be afraid to ask questions and always read the fine print. Some accounts have monthly service fees. Try to avoid them at all costs. However, if you must use one of those accounts, you can always get around the fees by having direct deposit over a certain amount which is determined by the bank. Do your research; many banks waive the service fee while you are in college.

Always sign up for overdraft protection. This protection deducts money from your savings and deposits funds to your checking to cover transactions that put you over the balance in your checking account. This will also help you avoid the $35 overdraft fee.

For example, if you buy a $5 cup of coffee but you only have $3 in your account, the bank will automatically transfer the $2 from your savings account to cover the transaction.

If you did not have overdraft protection, the bank may still approve the transaction, but they may charge you that $35 overdraft fee. So that same cup of coffee just cost you $37.

To avoid over-drafting your account, sign up for low balance text alerts. You can set the alert for any amount you desire, so you'll be notified when your account reaches a certain balance. Using this tool will help you save money and headache.

Action Steps

- Shop around for a bank that meets your needs.
- Get at least one checking and savings account set up.
- Avoid those monthly service charges, by having direct deposit or maintaining a balance set by the bank.
- Utilize the overdraft protection or just keep track of your spending.

Now That You Have a Job, this is What You Need to Know!

Welcome to the world of earning your own income. However, do not get used to the words "earned income." After reading this book, you should have a broader perspective on the different types of income that you can earn, and not be limited to just making money from your job. There are three types of income: earned/active income, portfolio income, and passive income.

Let's get into it.

Earned/active income is the exchange of time for money. This is typically the type of income earned from a job and a paycheck. If you have a job, and you are paid by the hour, you are only paid for the hours you work. If you cannot work, you don't get paid unless you use vacation days, sick days or paid time off (PTO) days.

Portfolio income is the income you receive from capital gains from stocks, bonds, and 401K. These assets involve patience and risk. It is almost like playing the lottery, but before you jump into this investment, always speak to an investment advisor.

In case you were wondering what stocks, bonds, and 401K's are, here is a quick crash course.

Stocks are shares from businesses or corporations raised by capital. So, if you want to purchase stock from a shoe brand you like for $32.00 a share, depending on how many shares you buy, you could eventually be considered a shareholder for that company. Over time, that stock could increase to $100 which gives you a $68 profit.

Bonds are debt that is made with an investor for cash in exchange for payouts of interest. If you purchase a bond from the government or a corporation (i.e. bank), you will be paid interest after the maturity date has been reached. For example, you purchase a $1,000 bond for a year. Once the one-year maturity date has been reached, you will receive your $1,000 back plus the interest you have accumulated during that year.

401k is a retirement savings plan. Typically, this is something an employer offers you automatically. You are enrolled in their plan when you accept their offer of employment. Now, not all companies have a 401k, but that is okay; you can get another retirement plan such as a traditional or Roth IRA (individual retirement plan) through an outside company. IRAs are a special retirement account that you fund with after-tax income.

Disclaimer: To learn more about these investments, please refer to a professional.

Passive income is money earned with minimal activity, such as real estate investing, royalties you receive from your intellectual property when you write a book, make a movie, design clothes or shoes, or any other creative work that you sell or license to a company for profit. Passive income is also the lowest-taxed form of income.

A quick note about buying property:

Once you are old enough to purchase a home, go for it. Many people think it is scary purchasing and owning a home, they think it is too much responsibility. I am not saying it will be all sunshine and rainbows, but homeownership has its perks, starting with your own space. Owning a home can also strengthen your credit score and be used as leverage to borrow against your home loan to purchase investments.

You can really generate income from purchasing a home and renting part of the house out to others while you live there too. The income you get from tenants who live in your property is passive. You can literally turn your home into a business. Rent out rooms to cover the mortgage but find responsible family members and friends to live with.

No, this does not mean parties all night and day; remember this is a business so treat it like one. Set guidelines to establish how the rent will be paid and rules and regulations for the property.

Imagine this: You purchase a home not too far from your college campus. It has three bedrooms, two bathrooms, and an unfinished basement. Identify your room and the other two rooms are to be rented by tenants.

If the mortgage on your home is $1,100 a month, your two tenants (also students) could rent a bedroom for $400 a month each. This means you only must cover the remaining $300 per month. However, you could find two responsible individuals willing to pay $300 a month just to sleep in your unfinished basement.

You supply the beds and the rest is history. Now you get to live for free and your mortgage is paid for by your tenants. Great!

You can continue using this method through college and adulthood. Keep this up and you may not need to work again. Your rental income could pay off the mortgage on that property. Once that is done, you can either sell it for a profit, have your tenants move out and you can start your own family in that house without a mortgage. Either is a great position to be in. With this mindset and smart moves, you are well on your way to building wealth.

Action Steps

Before you purchase a property, make sure you do the math. Estimate the monthly mortgage, then see how much rent you can generate each month. If you have a positive cash flow, go for it. Even if you break even, go for it. You would be living for free.

But if you have a negative cash flow, run from this property.

Home and Renters Insurance

I know having homeowner's or renter's insurance does not seem like a big deal, but it is. In fact, in most places, a lender (bank or financial institution) will not give you a loan unless you have homeowner's insurance. Homeowner's insurance covers the homeowner in case of fire, theft from the home, natural disasters and more.

You can specify in the policy things that are valuable to you such as wedding bands and jewelry to cover those items as well. It also covers liabilities when you have friends and family over and they accidentally get hurt on your property.

Renters insurance covers your personal property while you are renting a place from theft or vandalism and liability in case a visitor gets injured on the premises. Although you may think this is just another bill, look at it as protection. You may not get the full value for your property or belongings, but it is better than walking away empty-handed.

For example, let's say Michael is renting a three-bedroom home from a friend. The house was broken into and all his personal valuables were taken. Michael called his insurance carrier and an insurance adjuster came out to verify the documentation of the break-in and theft.

The adjuster verified police reports, the damage to the back door and receipts of the items taken. Thank goodness for insurance! Michael was able to recoup the cost of the things that were stolen. If Michael did not have renter's insurance, he would have taken a total loss on everything that was taken.

Action Steps

Once you purchase a property always keep your insurance up to date, never let it lapse. This applies to renter's and homeowner's insurance.

Live Debt Free

I know having a credit card sounds cool and it might be a great thing to have, but it is not the smartest choice. Credit cards should be used for emergencies only. An emergency is an unforeseen circumstance, which can be a car repair, losing your job and needing to survive, or a medical emergency. It does not mean the latest Jordan's or a new game system.

Your credit card is as important as having a driver's license. It is easy to get a credit card once you turn 18 and it is very easy to swipe and spend. However, you must have the discipline not to overspend. Just like a driver's license, once you have that beautiful shiny card with your picture, you have to keep it. Using your credit card recklessly can cost you hundreds, maybe thousands.

Credit card companies normally target young people in high school. Your first piece of mail will more than likely be that beautiful shiny pre-printed card with your name on it. A typical teenager would open the mail and activate their new card and start spending. However, not you - you are above average. If you choose to activate that card, you will use it for gas, groceries, and emergencies. No, hanging out with family and friends is not an emergency.

If you spend $80.00 that month, the key is to pay off the card before the end of the billing cycle. You will not be charged interest. Remember, it takes approximately three years to rebuild your credit if you are not mindful of spending.

Credit cards are tempting. Instead of using cards for emergencies, some rely on credit cards to bridge the gap between their paycheck and the money they need for expenses.

As many as 4 out of 10 people still seemingly cannot pay for necessities with their paychecks alone. That's leading some to embrace credit cards as a way out. According to a poll released earlier in 2019, not only did young people not have a few hundred dollars in their bank account, about 4 in 10 millennials have gone into credit card debt for day-to-day expenses like groceries, while 20 percent have accrued debt over sudden costs like car repairs or medical bills.

Data from the Federal Reserve that was released in 2018 revealed that about 40 percent of Americans would not be able to cover an emergency expense of approximately $400. Therefore, an emergency fund is essential. Credit cards are not a substitute for a savings account.

Always try to pay for things in cash, not credit. If you must use a credit card to purchase something, make sure you are able to pay off the purchase before the end of the billing cycle. Paying in cash keeps you out of debt and avoiding interest charges.

The longer you carry a balance on a card, the more interest that balance accrues. The interest will be tacked on to the balance, and if you are not careful, you can end up paying thousands of dollars more than your original purchase amount.

What is Interest?

In a nutshell, interest is a percentage you pay for holding a loan. You can think of this as a cost for borrowing money. You should avoid interest at all costs because it is an easy way to stay in debt. If you have a credit card or loan, pay off the card or loan before its due date. The interest could cost you hundreds, maybe even thousands of dollars. Another way to build a good credit rating is to always keep the debt you owe below 30%, never close a credit card and always pay more then what is owed. Creditors want to see you are responsible with debt and that you can control your spending. Therefore, having credit is necessary, but you must learn to handle the credit debt.

According to NerdWallet, "Paying just the minimum on your credit card balance means you'll pay more in interest. In fact, the average household with credit card debt pays a total of $1,292 in credit card interest per year."

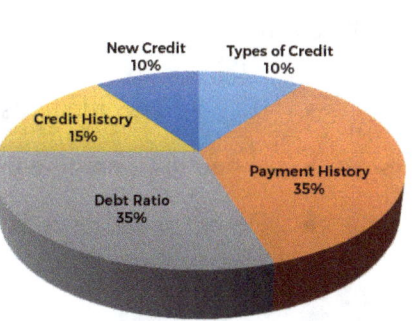

Fact: About 77 million Americans or 35 percent of adults with a credit file have debt in collections reported in their credit files, according to the Urban Institute.

How to Avoid Interest

The main way to avoid interest is to use cash, but if you have to use financed money, always pay on time and pay more than the monthly payment. If the monthly payment is $50, pay $75 so you can avoid the interest penalty. Paying early and more than the amount owed will lower the interest charge dramatically.

📌 *Do not go in debt for things you want… Sleep on it and give it a few days – delay gratification.*

Action Steps

Rule of thumb: If you do not have enough cash to buy an item three times, you should not buy it.

Ex. You see a pair of sneakers for $100. You have $75 in your account and $300 on your credit card. In this scenario, you do not have enough to purchase the sneakers. "Credit card" money is not *YOUR* money.

- If you do decide to use a credit card, use it responsibly.
- If you have credit cards, pay them to a zero balance.
- Do not spend over 30% of your overall balance.

Financial Independence

Financial independence is having enough income to pay your living expenses without having to work a full-time job. Sometimes that income is generated through real estate, stocks, or successful business ventures.

The best way to become a millionaire or maybe a billionaire is to achieve financial independence. Doesn't that sound great?

How would you like to be your own boss, travel the country, live on the beach, do everything you want to do, wake up surfing, swimming, and partying? It can be done with just a paradigm shift, making wise money moves, and managing your money well.

What holds many people back from financial freedom is their mindset. But you have the power to change this. You can change how you view, use, and make money and leave a legacy for the people coming behind you.

There are many ways to earn money, but let's start with profits.

"Wages make you a living, profits make you a fortune." Jim Rohn

If you are a business/company owner, or maybe a distributor of goods (a.k.a products), when consumers (a person who purchases goods and services for personal use) purchase your goods, the business makes a profit from the sales. It doesn't matter what age you are, whether you are dead or alive, the financial gain continues. However, as a person who makes wages (a.k.a an employee/earned income earner) the money only comes in when you work for an hourly or salary wage.

Action Steps

You can create a business and earn income from just about anything. Take an inventory of your talents and what you enjoy doing. Do you like baking cakes? Editing papers? Drawing or designing clothes? These are all services that people are willing to pay you for. Once you decide what you'd like to try, tell everyone you know about your new business and start making money!

In the process of starting a business, *do not* accumulate debt. Choose a business that you can start with as little money as possible. Buy the basic supplies you need to get a few customers. As you make money, reinvest a portion of that money back into your business.

Keep in mind that your goal is always financial independence. The less debt you have, the better. Your business should make you money, not increase your debt.

How to Grow Wealth

There are many ways to make money, but in this case, I am going to discuss the options I have knowledge in and that have proven to be successful for me.

One of the best ways to accumulate great wealth is through real estate. In case you are unaware, real estate has no minimum or maximum age requirement. You can start now.

Earlier in this section, I mentioned how you could earn income from purchasing a property, live in it, and rent other rooms to pay the mortgage so you could live for free. This is an ideal situation; you are still living at home with your parents. If you follow this strategy, you could be taking the first step to creating wealth to benefit you for years to come.

Let's look at how you actually purchase that property.

Let's get started!

Before you start hunting for a property:

1. Check your credit score. You will need a score of at least 630 to qualify for a loan.
2. Research mortgage companies.

3. Get a pre-approval letter from a lender of your choice (this would be a bank or credit union). Be sure to specify you want a rehab loan.

A pre-approval letter states the buyer can afford the property, providing you meet the necessary credit criteria when it's time to get approved for the loan.

Find the Right Property and Team

Once you have your pre-approval letter, you want to find a multi-unit building that needs work/rehab. It is very important that you run the numbers. What does that mean? Determine that the mortgage, utilities, maintenance costs, taxes, and insurance fit into your budget and you can maintain positive cash flow. If you can net at least $100 a month, you are looking at a great property.

Now that you have found your ideal property, contact a real estate agent who will help you with the purchase. Before you purchase make sure you have a contractor give you a pre-estimate on the repairs. This person can help you determine exactly how much renovation the property will need.

Making an Offer

Once you determine the property is what you want, it is time to make an offer. By this time, the realtor has told you about the comparable properties (or comps) in the area. Comps are other properties in your price range. This is important information to help you determine how much to offer for the property *(if you decide to fix and flip.)* Your offer should be within the range of the comps.

If you really want the property, you should offer the seller the full asking price, maybe a few thousand over. Also, put $1,000 of earnest money towards the deal to let the seller know you mean business. After the seller accepts your offer, bring in a contractor to give you a renovation quote (or a bid).

Always get three bids unless you are very familiar with this person. I would highly recommend asking around. The contractor will offer their bid and submit the quote to the lender. Once everything is approved, it is time to close on the property.

Purchasing Your Property

If you decide to live in the basement in your multi-level building, you will only need a 3% down payment of the overall price. That would be 3% of the entire loan. (i.e. property cost, renovations, taxes, and fees.)

Now that you have closed on the property and signed your life away (not really!), you are a homeowner, investor, and, soon, a landlord. Depending on the contractor, it could take approximately

6-9 months to renovate the property. This is okay because you are still living at home. Nonetheless, remember you will have a mortgage payment due 45 days after the property closes, so be sure to budget for that full amount.

You will have to cover the entire mortgage until the renovation is complete. But 6-9 months later, the property is everything you have envisioned. It is time to get tenants.

Do the Math

A three-unit building with you living in the basement:

- Mortgage: $1,200.00
- Three rental units at $1,000 = $3,000.00
- Net profit: $ 1,800.00 (not including repairs and maintenance)

In addition, you will be living for free in the basement. Think about repeating this for the next 10 years, and you could be close to financial independence by age 30.

House Hack

What is a house hack you ask? House hacking is what you did in the previous section. That is when you purchase a piece of property and you move in to prevent from paying the 20% down payment. When purchasing a property for your primary residence, it only requires a 3% down payment. In about three years when the property is rehabbed and ready to be sold, you could sell the property, move on to another property, and repeat this strategy.

Becoming a Real Estate Investor

- Have you watched any HGTV shows?
- Have you seen a boarded-up house turn into a gem?
- Have you wondered how people live in the nicest homes, with the most expensive cars?

If the answer to these questions is "yes", then you are in the right place.

A real estate investor is a person who invests in property, whether it is a buy and hold or a flip to a retail buyer. Buy and hold investors identify a property, then purchase it to rehab and rent the property out to a tenant. A tenant is a person who has the right to use the rental property in accordance with the lease agreement.

A flipper, on the other hand, is a person who purchases property to fix it and sell it to a retail buyer.

Retail buyers are purchasing a home for personal use, not as an investment.

There are pros and cons to owning real estate. However, if you are looking for financial freedom or want to be your own boss and spend more time with friends and family it is a great career. Or, if you want to get paid for helping people with affordable housing, being a real estate investor might be for you.

Don't get caught chasing money. Chase your passions, dreams, and aspirations. There is nothing wrong with a 9 to 5 job, I have one. However, use your job to fund your business ideas. The goal is to make the money work for you day and night. Yes, even while you sleep. Real estate investing can help you do that.

For example, a real estate investor has two properties that have a cash flow of $1,000 each month which is a total of $2,000.

If the real estate investor keeps a tenant in that property, they can make an extra $24,000 a year (minus the maintenance and taxes). The investor did not work hard for that extra $2,000. Additionally, having rental property is a tax deduction, which means all maintenance is deductible.

The most important part about having rental investments is being able to pass the property on to a family member who will reap the benefits.

A good rule of thumb is to have an investment property for every expense you have.

For instance, your expenses might be a car payment, cell phone bill, groceries, gas, and rent. Total each expense and find a property to cover those expenses.

Example: You have a $300 car payment and a $100 phone bill totaling $400. Find an investment property that nets you $400 per month. This will allow someone else to pay for your expenses.

Maybe you have a future expense that you have identified, such as college. Do the research to find out how much each semester will cost and find the investment property to pay the expenses. The plan will ease the stress of working night and day to pay for college. Let someone pay you to attend college.

Let's look at some real numbers so you can see the difference between the cash flow for an employee vs. an investor.

Sample Income Statement for An Employee

Figure 1

INCOME	EXPENSES
$800.00 a month earned income from working.	Car Payment: $250
	Groceries: $150
	Insurance: $125
	Cell Phone Bill: $125
	Gas: $75
	Eating and Hanging Out: $75

ASSETS	LIABILITIES
None	Car
	Jewelry
	Accessories
	Car accessories (Rims, car audio)
	Expensive cell phone

Sample Income Statement for An Investor

Figure 2

Income	Expenses
$800 from work	Car Payment: $250
$200 from stocks	Groceries: $150
$250 from #1 investment property	Insurance: $125
$250 from #2 investment property	Cell Phone Bill: $125
$100 from book royalties	Gas: $75
	Eating and Hanging Out: $75

Assets	Liabilities
Stocks	Car
Property#1	Jewelry
Property #2	Accessories
Royalties from book	Car accessories (Rims, car audio)
	Expensive cell phone

The figures above are what an income statement looks like. It shows the money coming in and the money going out. It's sort of like cash flow. In Figure 1, we see a person who has a monthly income of $800 but has expenses and liabilities that take away from the monthly earnings. This leaves the person in Figure 1 with a cash flow of $0 every month (He basically breaks even every month). Although there is no right or wrong way, Figure 2 shows a better way you can generate positive income.

Figure 2 shows a person generating $1600 per month from different streams of income. It also shows this person has the same expenses and liabilities as the person in Figure 1. The difference is the person in Figure 2 has additional income from stocks, properties, and royalties. In Figure 2's example, his monthly income is $1600, and his expenses are $800, which leaves him with a positive cash flow of $800.

This example is what every person should strive for; after all, expenses are paid, you will have money left over. The person in Figure 2 will still generate income from the assets, whether he works or not. He doesn't have to worry about how to pay his car note, cell phone, and other expenses. He can pay his expenses and still have income leftover.

Positives and The Negatives About Investing.

Becoming a real estate investor can be challenging and comes with headaches. You can overcome them all, but I want you to be prepared for exactly what you can expect.

Being a real estate investor could be risky if you are not protecting your assets. Having an LLC (Limited Liability Company) helps you to pass the liability to your company. In case of a lawsuit, your personal property will not be affected; only the assets listed in the LLC are in danger. Yes, it is a possibility to get sued, but you are minimizing the risk by having an LLC. The property is a business and must be treated like one.

You will have quarterly inspections, interactions with the tenants where you make sure their concerns are met, and you will have to treat your property and tenants with respect.

Occasionally, you might get a bad tenant who will damage the property. As a landlord, it is your responsibility to perform a thorough background check on every tenant. This background check could include work history, references, and previous and current landlords. Additionally, remember the section discussing social media earlier in the book? This is a good example where someone can view and check the possible tenant's social media to get an idea of what type of lifestyle the person lives.

You are the landlord. When a problem occurs, you, as a landlord, are the one responsible. This may include monetary payments for broken or damaged property or for an accident that occurred on your property *(but insurance should cover this.)*

For example: If your tenant has family or visitors over and they fall or trip on the porch due to the condition of old wood, they may look to sue you for neglecting the property and failing to make the porch safe for use. Again, this is another example of why having an LLC and quarterly safety checks are important.

If you have been filing a tax return every year, there will be a change. The income you receive from your property will put you in another tax bracket. It means you should prepare for the possibility of paying income taxes at the end of the year. You can also pay quarterly taxes to ease the owed amount during tax season. It is time to research tax deduction, depreciation, and eligible expenses.

Invest in Your Community

Once you own property in a neighborhood, it is important to invest in it.

Help build up your community by forming block clubs, phone trees and attend beat meetings. Beat meetings are those monthly meetings hosted by the police officers in your community. This helps create those positive community interactions and helps build a stronger and more trusted community.

Remember: You cannot spell the word community without "UNITY."

A community consists of everyone from you, your tenants, neighbors, police officers, firemen, nurses, business owners, teachers, mail carriers, children, teens, and even the gang members. Without any of these people, there is no community.

Ask yourself, "How involved am I in my community?" Can you make a difference? Yes, you can.

Here is how:

- Once a month, contact your city service department and have a block club clean-up. Use the city service department to cut the grass in an abandoned parking lot and replace streetlights. You and your community members can pick up trash and trim neighborhood bushes that might be a blind spot for people coming home at night.
- If you don't recognize a car on your block, call 911. This could be a stolen car or a car that has victims inside. Whatever the case, when in doubt, call 911. This will ensure that your neighborhood remains safe and crime-free.

- If you see abandoned homes with broken windows, call 911 to get these homes boarded up. This may not look like a huge deal, but it is. Abandoned homes can be used as trap houses, a place to commit sexual crimes or where homeless people sleep. These homes are a danger to the community. Work with police to have them properly secured to prevent danger or harm to any citizen.

📢 Trap house (slang) -a house where drugs are used and sold. This place could also be used to secure weapons and stolen merchandise and hide from "12," also known as the police.

- Start a social media page for your neighborhood. Post suspicious activities such as unknown cars, spots with high gang activity, etc. You can also use this platform to reach out to other volunteers who want to participate in the monthly clean-up activity.

No matter what, you are your own police. You don't have to wait to call the police to initiate positive change. You can help. Keep an eye out, always. When you are aware and watching the people around you (i.e. bad influences, suspicious people, etc.), you protect your family, friends, and neighborhood. You help others in their time of need and you contribute to making the community safe. This is what officers do. You can do the same.

Action Steps

Here are some additional ways to get involved with your community:

- Once a month, check-in with your local police department. Speak with the community policing office and ask if they have any volunteer activities you could participate in.
- Talk with people in the community and see what their needs are, or if there are any concerns in the neighborhood that need attention.
- Start a block club.

You Got This!

I wrote this book to help you change your perspective, and, hopefully, your life. I hope that you are reading this page with an open mind and an excitement for what possibilities exist for you.

There are so many paths you can take in this life. Choose the one that you want. Live your dreams. Create the life you see for yourself. You can have whatever you want—if you decide to go for it.

If you ask any adult you know, they will agree that the information that you have read in this book is what they wish they had known at your age. Much of what I shared here isn't typically learned until much later in life, if at all. A book like this would have helped many adults make better decisions, and to avoid many mistakes.

Personally, as a young man, I needed someone to teach me things about surviving and thriving in life. I needed to be introduced to new possibilities and ideas. I needed a book like this. So, I hope this book will help you the way it would have helped me. Reread it as many times as you need to. Let this information guide your life.

And remember, if you are chasing someone else's dreams or no dreams at all, you can change that today.

I hope that you will.

Whatever it is you choose to do, GIVE 110%

YOU GOT THIS!!!

Youth Pledge

I will be grateful for this day.

I will respect myself and others.

I will value myself.

I will help others.

I will be slow to anger.

I will strive to do my best in everything I do.

I will stay committed to my goals and aspirations.

My best is yet to come.

Positive Affirmations

I am beautiful/handsome.

I am happy with who I am.

I am in control of my actions.

I will respect others.

I am smart.

I am positive.

I am healthy.

I am grateful.

I am secure.

I am confident.

I am successful.

I am a blessed.

About the Author

Labeled an at-risk youth, Carmichael Lewis decided as a young man that he would not allow a rough start to define the trajectory of this life. So, he has not—and he is committed to ensuring that every young person who crosses his path can say the same.

Understanding early that education was key to expansion and growth, Carmichael is the only one of three siblings to attend college. He graduated from Chicago State University with a bachelor's degree in Criminal Justice, and he obtained a master's degree in Public Safety Administration from Calumet College of St. Joseph.

In 2012, Carmichael began his career with the Chicago Police Department. He has spent five of those years serving the south suburbs surrounding Chicago. He has received numerous awards and accolades for his service. During his adventures as a police officer, he encountered many disadvantaged youths in the community. Seeing himself in each of them, he felt called to do more. He volunteers at local high schools and grammar schools, empowering students and helping them unlock their optimal potential. Carmichael also serves as an instructor in a youth program created by the City Colleges of Chicago, Chicago Fire

Department, and Chicago Public Schools. This program offers classes to students interested in public safety careers. His role is to guide junior and senior students through the process of potentially becoming a police officer or firefighter. Whether it is mentoring or encouraging participants to pursue their goals by getting them physically healthy for their careers, Carmichael receives insurmountable joy from the experience.

When he is not working with youth, Carmichael is serving others through one of his other primary passions, physical fitness. He became a certified personal trainer so that he could help people look and feel their best. With his fitness company, he influences everyday people to achieve their ideal lifestyle through physical and mental wellness. As a health advocate, Carmichael knows the power of a fit body and actively promotes regular exercise to reduce the risk of disease and increase life expectancy.

Although Carmichael faced many setbacks in life, he managed to escape the traps of negativity and create a life for himself that he is undeniably proud of. Now, as an author, he is on a mission to help young people everywhere to learn from his mistakes, grow from his successes, and become a person we can all be proud of.

Join us in empowering and transforming lives through our dynamic programs designed to inspire growth, foster resilience, and build a stronger community.

Through our transformative programs, we equip young men with essential life skills, foster meaningful connections with mentors and role models, and create opportunities for personal growth and success. From our Men's Circle facilitating healing and leadership to our Male Mentoring program offering guidance and support, each initiative is thoughtfully designed to empower participants and unlock their full potential.

Explore our diverse range of programs designed to empower young men. From our Men's Circle fostering healing and leadership to our Male Mentoring program, each initiative is carefully crafted to empower participants and nurture their potential.

Visit us at youthandblueunited.com

To learn more about the author visit Carmichaellewis.com

Notes

Additional Books from the Author
carmichaellewis.com

Shadows of the Past- *The Path to Greatness*

ISBN: 978-1733555135 Paperback
ISBN: 9781648731259 Epub

Julian Parker never prepared himself for the moment that this incredible woman would have walked into his life. Aniyah's presence captivated his soul from the second they met. By their first date, he knew she would be the perfect mate. People always mock love at first sight, but to Julian the disbelief was false. Julian had spent much of his adulthood running from the past, fighting to free himself from the incidents that had plagued his life.

The newlyweds planned an incredible trip to Hawaii for their honeymoon, and it was an exhilarating time for both parties. Neither one had traveled much, so experiencing the event together made the trip more worthwhile. But then the unthinkable happened. Aniyah sat in a hospital room, watching an artificial machine breathe for her husband. The last thing she wanted was to think about traveling when the love of her life was in the hospital.

In the months that follow, joy takes over: Aniyah and Julian celebrate their incredible news. It's as if Julian's heart condition doesn't exist. They want to drag out the experience indefinitely. Julian feels alive for the first time in his life. During chaos, the couple finds happiness within the smallest package: a baby girl is on the way. As Julian faces the imminent possibility of death, it allows him to dig deep within his soul and confess the overwhelming events of his past. In return, he learns true love is unconditional.

Mira Mira – Look!

ISBN: 9781647864194 Hardcover
ISBN: 9781647869908 Paperback
ISBN: 9781648731402 Epub

Mira Mira-Look! shows how our household is teaching our son English and Spanish at the same time. By having a Hispanic mother and a black father, our son is learning how we are unique from traditional families.

Mira Mira- Look! teaches children a few common words they see daily. It introduces a second language and shows that children's curiosity sparks them to inquire about their environment... saying "Mira-Mira" in Spanish or "Look" in English. From our household to yours, we hope you enjoy Mira Mira- Look!

www.ingramcontent.com/pod-product-compliance
Lightning Source LLC
Chambersburg PA
CBHW072006110526
44592CB00012B/1219